T0237672

MonoGame Mastery

Build a Multi-Platform 2D Game and Reusable Game Engine

Jarred Capellman
Louis Salin

Apress®

MonoGame Mastery

Jarred Capellman
Cedar Park, TX, USA

Louis Salin
Cedar Park, TX, USA

ISBN-13 (pbk): 978-1-4842-6308-2
https://doi.org/10.1007/978-1-4842-6309-9

ISBN-13 (electronic): 978-1-4842-6309-9

Copyright © 2020 by Jarred Capellman, Louis Salin

This work is subject to copyright. All rights are reserved by the Publisher, whether the whole or part of the material is concerned, specifically the rights of translation, reprinting, reuse of illustrations, recitation, broadcasting, reproduction on microfilms or in any other physical way, and transmission or information storage and retrieval, electronic adaptation, computer software, or by similar or dissimilar methodology now known or hereafter developed.

Trademarked names, logos, and images may appear in this book. Rather than use a trademark symbol with every occurrence of a trademarked name, logo, or image we use the names, logos, and images only in an editorial fashion and to the benefit of the trademark owner, with no intention of infringement of the trademark.

The use in this publication of trade names, trademarks, service marks, and similar terms, even if they are not identified as such, is not to be taken as an expression of opinion as to whether or not they are subject to proprietary rights.

While the advice and information in this book are believed to be true and accurate at the date of publication, neither the authors nor the editors nor the publisher can accept any legal responsibility for any errors or omissions that may be made. The publisher makes no warranty, express or implied, with respect to the material contained herein.

Managing Director, Apress Media LLC: Welmoed Spahr
Acquisitions Editor: Spandana Chatterjee
Development Editor: Rita Fernando
Coordinating Editor: Divya Modi

Cover designed by eStudioCalamar

Cover image designed by Pixabay

Distributed to the book trade worldwide by Springer Science+Business Media New York, 1 New York Plaza, Suite 4600, New York, NY 10004-1562, USA. Phone 1-800-SPRINGER, fax (201) 348-4505, e-mail orders-ny@springer-sbm.com, or visit www.springeronline.com. Apress Media, LLC is a California LLC and the sole member (owner) is Springer Science + Business Media Finance Inc (SSBM Finance Inc). SSBM Finance Inc is a **Delaware** corporation.

For information on translations, please e-mail booktranslations@springernature.com; for reprint, paperback, or audio rights, please e-mail bookpermissions@springernature.com.

Apress titles may be purchased in bulk for academic, corporate, or promotional use. eBook versions and licenses are also available for most titles. For more information, reference our Print and eBook Bulk Sales web page at http://www.apress.com/bulk-sales.

Any source code or other supplementary material referenced by the author in this book is available to readers on GitHub via the book's product page, located at www.apress.com/978-1-4842-6308-2. For more detailed information, please visit http://www.apress.com/source-code.

Printed on acid-free paper

To my wife, Amy, for always supporting me through thick and thin.
—Jarred Capellman

To my kids, in the hope that they pursue their dreams.
—Louis Salin

Table of Contents

About the Authors

Jarred Capellman has been professionally developing software for over 14 years and is Director of Engineering at SparkCognition in Austin, Texas. He started making QBasic text–based games when he was 9 years old. He learned C++ a few years later before studying OpenGL with the eventual goal of entering the gaming industry. Though his goal of professionally developing games didn't come to fruition, he continued deep diving into frameworks such as MonoGame, Vulkan, and DirectX as an important part of his free time. When not programming, he enjoys writing music and is working on his DSc in Cybersecurity, focusing on applying machine learning to security threats.

Louis Salin has been a developer for more than 15 years in a wide variety of fields, developing on Windows in the early days in C, C++, and eventually C# before working as a developer on Linux-based web applications using different scripting languages, such as Ruby and Python. His early love for coding comes from all the time he spent as a kid copying video games written in Basic from books borrowed from the library. He wrote his first game in high school and took many classes in computer graphics.

About the Technical Reviewer

Simon Jackson is a long-time software engineer and architect with many years of Unity game development experience, as well as an author of several Unity game development titles. He loves to both create Unity projects and lend a hand to help educate others, whether it's via a blog, vlog, user group, or major speaking event.

His primary focus at the moment is with the XRTK (Mixed Reality Toolkit) project; this is aimed at building a cross-platform Mixed Reality framework to enable both VR and AR developers to build efficient solutions in Unity and then build/distribute them to as many platforms as possible.

Acknowledgments

There were two big drivers for bringing me to focus my career on programming. The first being my father who handed me a QBasic book when I was 9 years old. He supported my passion for programming throughout my childhood, buying books and updated versions of Visual Basic and Visual C++ every release. The other was John Carmack. When I first played *Wolfenstein 3D* in 1992, I was mesmerized at how immersive the game was. A few years later seeing John Carmack on the cover of the *Wired* magazine, reading how he and John Romero had created and transformed the first-person-shooter genre, I knew I wanted to achieve that level of impact in my career.

—Jarred Capellman

Many events in my life brought me to this point, where I get to thank the people who have helped me and believed in me. My father bought me my first computer and enrolled me in a Basic class in sixth grade, where I learned how to draw lines and circles on the screen.

Years later, Richard Egli, my computer graphics professor in college, brought me to my first SIGGRAPH conference where I learned how deep the rabbit hole goes. Thank you for believing in me.

Finally, I'd like to thank Jarred, my coauthor, for giving me a chance to help him write this very book.

—Louis Salin

Introduction

Building video games has an undeniable appeal in the imagination of many people coming from various backgrounds. Many children want to be game designers when they grow up and many programmers have learned the art of writing code thinking that they would, one day, create their own game.

Creating a video game is both an expressive art form and a series of logical challenges that must be solved. A game programmer needs to be creative while materializing the content of their imagination on a computer monitor, and at the same time, they must constantly solve the many physical constraints placed upon them as they shape their game. For those of us that enjoy solving problems and have a penchant for art, this is a dream field, whether as a hobby or, professionally, as a full-time job.

There has never been a better time for regular people than today to write video games! While hobbyists around the world have built games since the 1970s, the amount of deep technical knowledge required has diminished and the barrier of entry has dropped much lower in the last few years. Game tooling and game engines now abstract away the complexities of getting something drawn on a screen, while computers have gotten so powerful that programmers do not have to be so precise anymore in the way they handle memory management and the game performance. Furthermore, getting a video game published on gaming consoles and computers has become much more accessible today to anyone with the perseverance to bring their game to completion, as can be seen with the sheer number of indie games found on the market.

Software developers today have a wide array of technologies to choose from when building their game. One of these choices is MonoGame, a framework for creating powerful cross-platform games.

INTRODUCTION

In this book, we aim to take experienced C# programmers through a journey as we explain game development basics and build a small two-dimensional vertical shooter video game from scratch, using MonoGame as our framework. By the end of this book, our readers will not only have built a reusable game engine that they will be able to use in their future games, but they will also have gained valuable knowledge to give them a leg up in their future projects, whatever framework or engine they decide to use.

CHAPTER 1

Introduction

Chances are by reading this opening line you are at the very least intrigued to start learning about developing a game from scratch. This book was written to take you from this thought to fruition utilizing the MonoGame Framework. We will start by providing you, the reader, a strong foundation in the MonoGame architecture and continuing through with sprites, sound, and collision detection before wrapping up with separation of concerns preparing you for future developments.

Unlike other books on game development, this book will evolve with each chapter building on the last with a project-based approach as opposed to snippets of code here and there. For this book we will start from scratch on a vertical shooter akin to those of the late 1980s and early 1990s. The vertical shooter game type is a great starting point for aspiring game developers as it contains all the elements found in modern games:

- Multilayered scrolling backgrounds

- Collision detection of projectiles and enemies

- Computer-controlled enemies

- Sprites

- Player input

- Event-based sound effects

- Level structure

© Jarred Capellman, Louis Salin 2020
J. Capellman and L. Salin, *MonoGame Mastery*,
https://doi.org/10.1007/978-1-4842-6309-9_1

In addition, this book will dive into proper engine design and game tooling that are arguably overlooked in many game development books.

In this chapter, you will learn about

- MonoGame at a high level

- Difference between MonoGame and game engines

- Game types suited to MonoGame

- What to expect from the book and previews of the chapters to come

Who This Book Is For?

This book is targeting the aspiring game developer who wants to make a 2D game. Royalty-free game assets for sound, music, textures, and sprites will be provided (all created by yours truly), thus allowing the book to focus on the programming and architecture components of game development without worrying about cranking out game assets.

What This Book Is Not

While we will review game types as it relates to what pairs well with MonoGame, this book will not go over game design principles, asset creation, or the game development life cycle. There are numerous resources available including entire books devoted to these individual components and are outside the scope of this book.

Reader Assumptions

While no game development experience is required, there is an expectation that you are a seasoned C# programmer. While MonoGame is easy to get started with due to the architecture and the simple design, the framework is written in C#. In addition, the project we will be iterating on throughout this book utilizes many core aspects of the C# programming language such as inheritance and reflection. If you find yourself reviewing the accompanied source code and are struggling, I suggest picking up *C# Programming for Absolute Beginners* also from Apress to close the gaps.

From a development machine standpoint, this book will review how to configure a MonoGame development environment on both macOS and Windows with Visual Studio. Linux can also be used as a development environment with Visual Studio Code; however, Windows will be the preferred environment for the scope of this book due to the tooling Visual Studio for Windows offers.

With all of the assets provided with this book in formats MonoGame's pipeline can natively read (more on this feature in Chapter 5), no other tools are required. Experience with tools such as Photoshop, 3ds Max, and Audition will come in handy for your future development efforts even if it is simply a beginner skill level.

At the time of this writing, version 3.8 of MonoGame is the latest production version available, which was released on August 10, 2020. This version will be used for all code samples and snippets throughout this book. Versions 3.8.x or later may be available by the time you are reading this; however, based on the road map, samples should continue to work without issue.

What Is MonoGame

MonoGame at the highest level is a C# Framework that provides the developer a canvas to quickly create the game of their dreams. MonoGame is open source (Microsoft Public License) and royalty-free (over 1000 games have been published to various stores). While MonoGame does offer 3D support, the community by and large uses its powerful 2D support almost exclusively, and that will be the focus in this book (for 3D games the use of Unity or Unreal Engine is recommended). MonoGame's source code is available on GitHub (`https://github.com/MonoGame/MonoGame`).

Like many frameworks and engines available today, MonoGame like C# is cross-platform. MonoGame currently runs on

- Windows Desktop (7/8.x/10)

- Universal Windows Platform

- MacOS

- Linux

- PlayStation 4

- Xbox One

- Nintendo Switch

- Android (4.2 or later)

- iOS

For PlayStation 4, Xbox One, and Nintendo Switch, it should be noted that additional developer agreements are required before publishing to the respective stores.

Given MonoGame's underlying usage of C#, as new platforms become supported by C#, MonoGame should not be far behind.

Throughout the book, we will review any platform-specific considerations such as resolution and input methods (touch vs. keyboard, for instance). Fortunately, designing around a cross-platform game does not require much upfront effort with MonoGame.

MonoGame at a high level provides

- The Main Game Loop

  - Handling Updates

  - Rendering Method

- Content Manager

- Content Pipeline

- Support for OpenGL and DirectX

One of the best features of MonoGame's design is this simplicity, unlike other frameworks that have an extremely difficult learning curve to even get the first pixel rendered. Over the course of this book, we will extend this structure to support more complex scenarios and provide a rich expandable engine to not only build on with each chapter but also provide a framework to build your own game. In Chapter 3, we will deep dive into this architecture.

Seasoned developers at this point may be wondering what the relationship between MonoGame and Microsoft's XNA framework is. At a high level, there isn't a direct relationship. The underlying structure bulleted earlier is retained and the use of C# as the language is where the correlations end. MonoGame grew out of a desire from Jose Antonio Leal de Farias in 2009 to create XNA Touch. Similar to the effort on Mono Touch to bring Mono to iOS, the goal was to bring XNA to iOS. By that point, XNA was stagnating with the release of 4.0 in 2010 (which would be the last version released) and an official statement ending support in 2013. From there XNA Touch was renamed to MonoGame with support coming to Android, Mac, and Linux shortly thereafter. MonoGame eventually made it to GitHub and at the time of this writing has over 2200 forks with 267 contributors.

MonoGame Compared to Engines

MonoGame as mentioned is a pure framework. From the beginning of development, the goals of MonoGame were to create a flexible, simple, but powerful framework. The main design reason for this was to allow MonoGame to be used in a wide range of genres and game types as opposed to an engine that more often than not is tailored to a specific genre (generally the genre that the game driving the engine's development was such as the *Quake* series).

An engine conversely like that of Unity, Unreal Engine, or id Tech, to name a few, provides an end-to-end engine and editor with all of the various components that make up a game engine such as rendering, physics, level editors, and content pipelines with integrations into modeling programs. Depending on the level of deviation from the engine's core, there may be very little for an implementer to have to extend on their own. The engine approach allows a team of artists and designers a canvas ready to start implementing the game as opposed to waiting for the programmers to create the engine from scratch or build on top of a framework such as MonoGame. Learning curves and licensing fees of the aforementioned engines also should be taken into consideration.

If you're reading this book, chances are you wish to dive a bit lower level with a quick learning curve – this book should achieve that.

Game Types Best Suited for MonoGame

As mentioned previously, MonoGame is best suited for 2D games. With the revival of classics from the 1980s and 1990s in addition to a return to simple but fun games like *Castle Crashers*, this isn't a hindrance, if anything a benefit as the framework is set up for these game types.

MonoGame can be used in a wide range of game types; the following are a few examples of types that work best. In addition, for each game type, the pros and cons in comparison to the other types will be reviewed. When planning a game, weighing all of the pros/cons of a particular type should be a major part of your development efforts. For your first game after completion of this book, choosing an easier to implement game type is strongly suggested.

Vertical Shooters

Popularized by Capcom's *1942* and enhanced into the 1990s as graphics and gameplay advancements were made, vertical shooters can range from more science-fiction ala *Major Stryker* or more grounded like that of *Raptor*. As mentioned earlier in this chapter, for this book we will be building a vertical shooter from the ground up; a screenshot of the game from Chapter 4 is depicted in Figure 1-1.

Figure 1-1. *Our 2D game from Chapter 4*

There are some advantages and disadvantages to developing vertical shooters:

Pros

- Easy to dive into.

- Controls are basic.

- Graphics are easy to implement.

- Level generation and tooling is simple.

- AI is easy to implement.

Cons

- Tired genre

  - Need to generate some unique gameplay to differentiate from *Raptor* and other well-known vertical shooters.

Horizontal Shooters

Made popular by games like *Einhander* in the 1990s, similar to a vertical shooter, but affords more variety in the gameplay. A great MonoGame example of this is Pumpkin Games' *Paladin* in Figure 1-2.

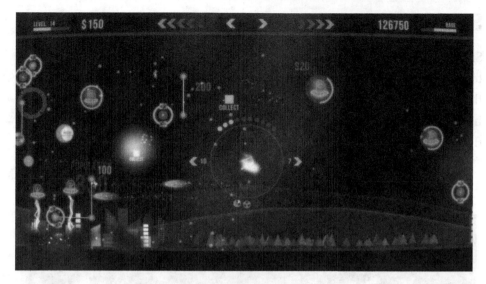

Figure 1-2. *Pumpkin Games' Paladin*

There are some advantages and disadvantages to developing horizontal shooters:

Pros

- Easy to dive into.

- Controls are basic.

- Level generation and tooling is simple.

- AI is easy to implement.

Cons

- Graphics fidelity in this genre is required to be high due to competition.

- Tired genre

  - Need to generate some unique gameplay to differentiate from other games.

9

Side Scrollers

Side scrollers are a genre that took off in the late 1980s and continues to this day, offering a wide range of adventure and action games from the horizontal perspective. MonoGame's native support for sprites and hardware-accelerated 2D graphics have made this an easy choice to develop for.

Krome Studios' *Tasmanian Tiger 4* is a great example of fluid animation and fast action using MonoGame as shown in Figure 1-3.

Figure 1-3. *Krome Studios' Tasmanian Tiger 4*

There are some advantages and disadvantages to developing side scrollers:

Pros

- Diverse Gameplay is achievable.

Cons

- Graphics can be tricky to implement depending on the gameplay.

- AI can also be tricky depending on the gameplay.

- Tooling can also be cumbersome to develop for.

Role Playing

Made popular by the *Final Fantasy* series on Super Nintendo, the 2D isometric view has been used ever since for 2D role-playing games. A popular example of this game type with MonoGame is ConcernedApe's *Stardew Valley* as shown in Figure 1-4.

Figure 1-4. *ConcernedApe's Stardew Valley*

Pros

- Diverse Gameplay is achievable.

- AI can be easy to implement (depending on the level of NPC interactions).

11

Cons

- Graphics handling of the tiles and sprites can be cumbersome.

- Tooling can also be cumbersome to develop for.

Puzzle

Puzzle games especially on mobile given the popularity of *Angry Birds* and *Bejeweled* among others in recent years coupled with MonoGame's ease of use are a perfect fit. An example of this game type using MonoGame is Endi Milojkoski's *Raining Blobs* as shown in Figure 1-5.

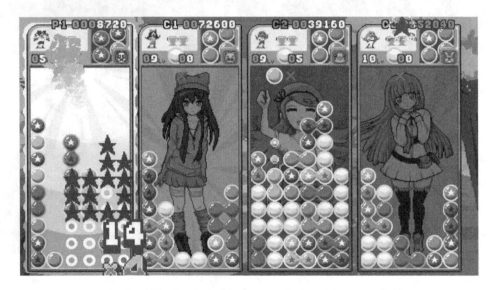

Figure 1-5. *Endi Milojkoski's Raining Blobs*

Pros

- Diverse Gameplay is achievable.

- Graphics can be easy to implement.

- AI can be easy to implement.

- Tooling can also be easy to implement.

Cons

- Achieving a unique and/or fun gameplay in the crowded market can be extremely challenging.

Strategy

Strategy games commonly range between turn-based, real-time, and strategy/role-playing game hybrids. While much more complex to design and implement, they can provide a unique experience for gamers. Reason Generator Inc's *Wayward Terran Frontier* is a good example of utilizing MonoGame to its fullest in Figure 1-6.

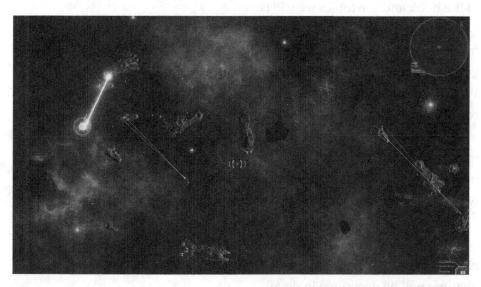

Figure 1-6. *Reason Generator Inc's Wayward Terran Frontier*

Pros

- Diverse Gameplay is achievable.

Cons

- Graphics can be tricky to implement depending on the gameplay.

- AI can also be tricky depending on the gameplay.

- Tooling can also be cumbersome to develop for.

Organization of This Book

As stated at the start of this chapter, this book breaks down each of the topics into manageable and isolated chapters. The following is an overview of the book and the topics we will cover:

Chapter 2 details how to get your development environment setup from start to finish for the remainder of the book. By the end of the chapter, you will be able to run a blank MonoGame project. Both macOS and Windows setup will be covered in detail. Linux will be discussed, but not recommended going forward for the rest of the book.

Chapter 3 deep dives into the MonoGame architecture including going into detail about 2D graphics, the game timer, and input. This chapter should not be overlooked even if you have done game development in the past as it will offer a deep insight into how MonoGame's architecture is set up.

Chapter 4 starts the deep dive into creating an architecture that we will be building off of for the remainder of the book. As with Chapter 3, this chapter should not be skipped as the objects, managers, and Game class changes will be described in detail.

Chapter 5 goes into detail of how the Asset pipeline works in MonoGame. In addition, integration with the ContentManager into the Game States will also be detailed. At the end of the chapter, we will render our first sprite.

Chapter 6 covers the handling of input with both a keyboard and mouse. In addition, platform-specific considerations will be reviewed to handle gamepad and touch screen input.

Chapter 7 goes into how to add audio to our architecture and add audio triggers to our event system. In addition, supporting background music layers will also be discussed.

Chapter 8 deep dives into how to integrate particles into our architecture to handle the bullet fire from both our player object and setup for future enemy objects.

Chapter 9 reviews various methods of collision detection used in games. For our project, we will use box collision and integrate it into our architecture to handle not only player object collisions but also projectile collisions.

Chapter 10 adds animations into our architecture and reviews approaches used throughout the industry. At the end of the chapter, animations of objects are added to the game.

Chapter 11 reviews the importance of level design and goes into detail of how to add level loading to our game engine.

Code Samples

Code samples starting with Chapter 3 will be referenced throughout each section. Outside of the code samples, there is also an Assets archive that contains all of the music, sound effects, sprites, and graphics used throughout the book.

Summary

In this chapter, you learned what MonoGame is exactly and the differences between MonoGame and game engines. In addition, you learned about game types that lend themselves to MonoGame and the book's chapter structure.

Up next is setting up your development environment to begin your MonoGame development.

CHAPTER 2

Configuring the Dev Environment

Now that the initial introduction to MonoGame is out of the way, we are ready to begin coding right? Not quite – we need to set up our development environment first in Visual Studio. Thankfully, over the years, this has become a much more streamlined process and will not take much time. In addition, configuring Linux for MonoGame development will be reviewed; however, as mentioned in Chapter 1, Windows will be used for all screenshots and included sample code.

Like most developments, a single tool can be used for development, but there are additional tools, plug-ins, and extensions to improve productivity. To help on your journey at the end of this chapter, I will review several tools that help me with both game and regular development.

In this chapter, you will

- Learn how to set up your development environment (Windows, macOS, and Linux)

- Review and suggest a few additional tools

- Review and suggest Visual Studio extensions

© Jarred Capellman, Louis Salin 2020
J. Capellman and L. Salin, *MonoGame Mastery*,
https://doi.org/10.1007/978-1-4842-6309-9_2

Development Environment Configuration

Platform Agnostic

Regardless of the platform being used, all of the packages are found on www.monogame.net/downloads/. As mentioned in Chapter 1, at the time of this writing, version 3.8 is used for all of the coding examples. If by the time you are reading this there is a later version and run into issues running the samples, please install 3.8.0.1641.

You can download MonoGame 3.8 here: https://github.com/MonoGame/MonoGame/releases/tag/v3.8.

Set Up Your Windows Development Environment

The first requirement on Windows is to install Visual Studio. For the samples in this book, Visual Studio 2019 Professional Edition (Version 16.7.2) is utilized. The community edition is freely available on https://visualstudio.microsoft.com/. When installing, be sure to install the *.NET desktop development* as shown in Figure 2-1. If you are planning on targeting UWP or mobile targets, also install the *Universal Windows Platform development* and *Mobile development with .NET*, respectively.

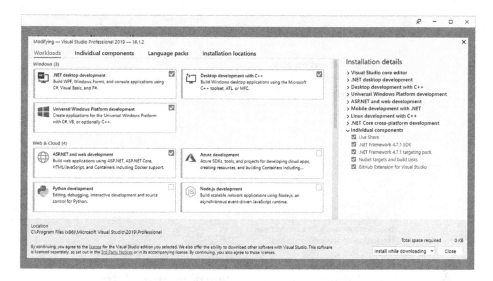

Figure 2-1. *Visual Studio installer*

I would strongly suggest installing Visual Studio on a SSD or NVMe drive (if available) as running Visual Studio especially the MonoGame compiling process is significantly slower on a traditional mechanical disk. In addition, make sure to have at least 8gb of RAM available.

After Visual Studio 2019 has been installed, on the downloads page mentioned earlier, click *MonoGame 3.8 for Visual Studio* from the previously referenced GitHub link. After downloading the MonoGame template installer for MonoGame (specifically MonoGame.Templates. CSharp.3.8.0.1641.vsix was used for the following screenshots in Figures 2-2 through 2-5), there are a few screens to get through. These are detailed in the following.

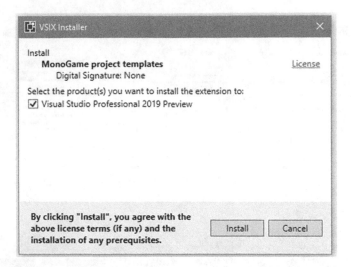

Figure 2-2. *MonoGame for Windows template installation*

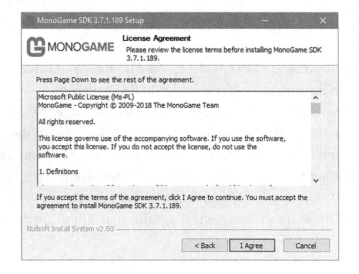

Figure 2-3. *License Agreement*

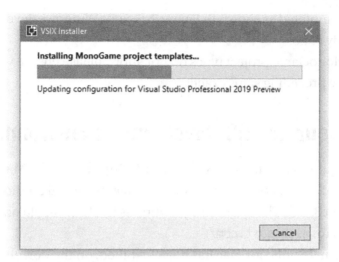

Figure 2-4. *Installing the project templates*

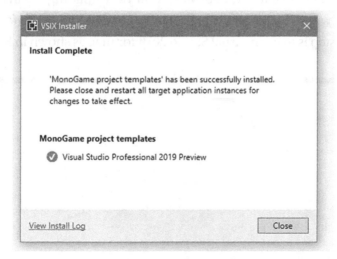

Figure 2-5. *MonoGame templates installed*

A major change in 3.8 compared to previous releases was the switch from a traditional installer in favor of NuGet packages and a simple vsix installation for the templates.

You only need to select Visual Studio 2017 even when using Visual Studio 2019 (the specific support is targeted in the next release).

Once completed as shown in Figure 2-5, your Windows development is almost ready to go.

If the MonoGame project types do not show, please ensure you followed the preceding steps exactly.

Set Up Your macOS Development Environment

The first requirement on macOS is to install Visual Studio for Mac. The samples used in this book have been tested against Visual Studio 2019 for mac (version 8.7.4). The community edition is freely available on `https://visualstudio.microsoft.com/`.

After Visual Studio for mac has been installed, on the downloads page mentioned earlier, click the download prefixed with MonoDevelop. MonoGame_IDE_VisualStudioForMac. After downloading the installer, there are a few screens to get through. These are detailed in the following.

The first step is to open Visual Studio 2019 for mac as shown in Figure 2-6.

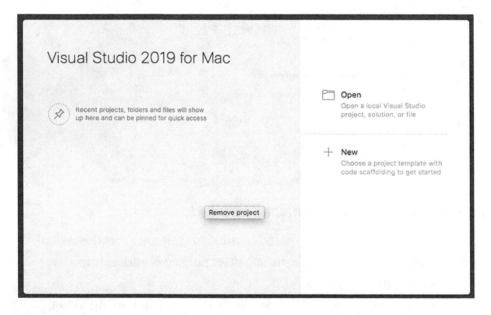

Figure 2-6. *Initial Visual Studio 2019 for mac screen*

From this screen, browse to the top menu and select Extensions as shown in Figure 2-7.

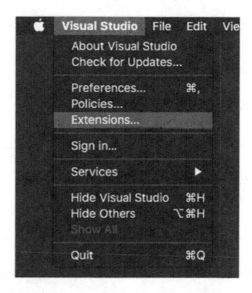

Figure 2-7. *Visual Studio 2019 for menu showing the Extensions selection*

After selecting Extensions, the Extension Manager will be shown as depicted in Figure 2-8.

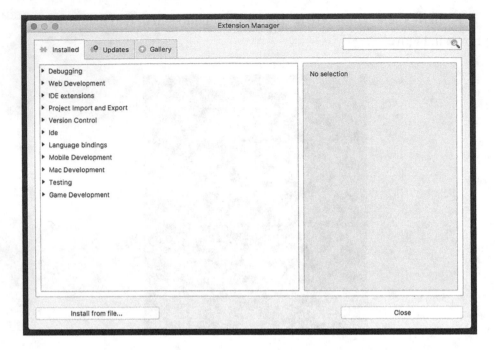

Figure 2-8. *Visual Studio 2019 for mac showing the Extension Manager*

Click Install from file..., which will open the file selection window like that shown in Figure 2-9.

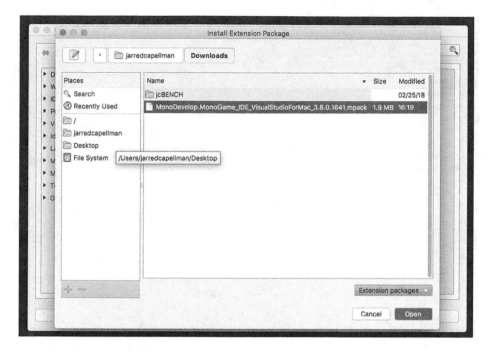

Figure 2-9. *Visual Studio 2019 for mac Extension file selection window*

From this window, browse for where you had downloaded the mpack file in the first step. Upon clicking Open after selection, a confirmation window will appear as shown in Figure 2-10.

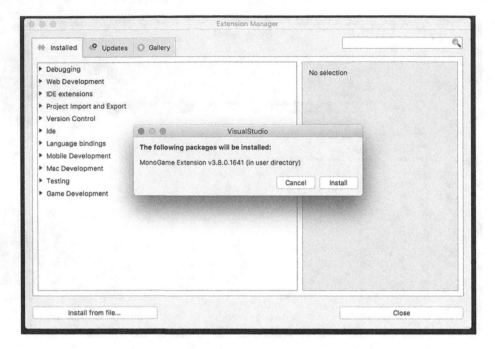

Figure 2-10. *Visual Studio 2019 for mac MonoGame Extension confirmation*

After a few moments, the installation will complete. Click the Close button to close the Extension Manager. Upon creating a new project, you will now see MonoGame templates as shown in Figure 2-11.

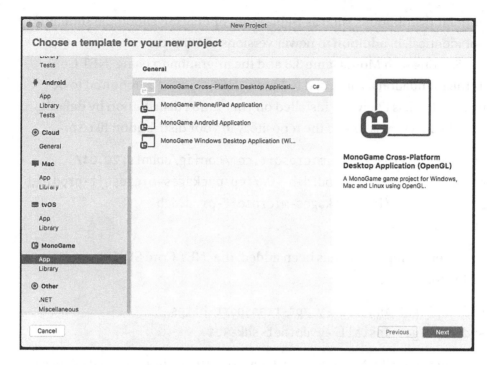

Figure 2-11. *Visual Studio 2019 for mac showing the MonoGame*
templates

Congratulations, your macOS development machine is now configured
for use with MonoGame!

Set Up Your Linux Development Environment

For Linux development, Visual Studio Code will need to be used. Visual
Studio Code is an open source editor that works across Windows, macOS,
and Linux.

The first step is to download Visual Studio Code from https://
code.visualstudio.com/. At the time of this writing, 1.48.0 is the latest
production build and is the version that will be used for the rest of this
book. In addition, Ubuntu 18.04 LTS will be used as the distribution. Other

popular distributions such as Debian and openSUSE should be similar if not identical, in addition to newer versions of Ubuntu.

Starting with MonoGame 3.8 and the migration to using .NET Core as the foundation as opposed to Mono, .NET Core 3.1 is required to be installed as it is likely not installed on your Linux distribution by default.

The first step is to add the repository to your distribution like so:

```
wget https://packages.microsoft.com/config/ubuntu/20.04/
packages-microsoft-prod.deb -O /tmp/packages-microsoft-prod.deb
sudo dpkg -i /tmp/packages-microsoft-prod.deb
sudo apt update
```

After the repository has been added, the .NET Core SDK can be installed:

```
sudo apt-get install -y apt-transport-https
sudo apt-get install -y dotnet-sdk-3.1
```

You can verify .NET Core's installation by executing a *dotnet --info* call on the terminal.

After .NET Core 3.1 is installed, calling the following will install the MonoGame templates:

```
dotnet new --install MonoGame.Templates.CSharp
```

After installation, your environment will be set up to develop on Linux.

Additional Tooling

Just having Visual Studio and MonoGame will be enough to get you started on your path toward creating a game and to follow along with this book; however, there are several tools and Visual Studio extensions to accelerate and enhance the development process. The following are some of the tools I use daily for both my general and game development.

Tools

Source Control Tools

GitHub (Windows, macOS, Linux)

There are several free tools I strongly suggest installing in addition to Visual Studio and MonoGame. One of the first things I would suggest however is creating a GitHub account (`https://github.com`). Since the Microsoft purchase of GitHub, private repositories are free and will provide you, as an iterative developer, source control for your work. In addition, recent additions to provide free CI/CD (continuous integration and continuous deployment) make the platform even more attractive for open source projects.

TortoiseGit (Windows Only)

While Visual Studio offers built-in Git support, I prefer the open source project TortoiseGit (`https://tortoisegit.org/`). The side-by-side diff tools, merge conflict resolution, and Windows Explorer integration I find do provide a better source control experience in addition to giving me an additional review process away from Visual Studio prior to a pull request or commit. See Figure 2-12.

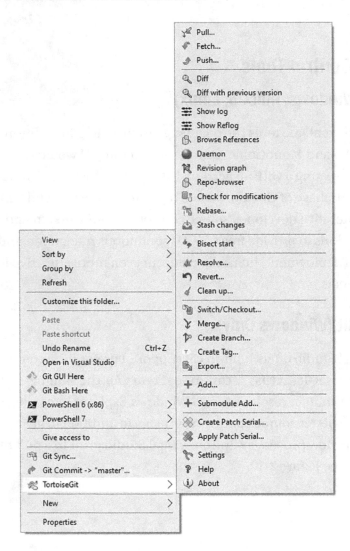

Figure 2-12. *TortoiseGit Windows Explorer Context Menu*

Graphics Tools

Blender (Windows, macOS, Linux)

While there are several 3D modeling applications available, Blender (`www.blender.org/`), version 2.8 at the time of this writing, is an excellent free 3D modeling and animation package. In addition, Blender supports many file formats for both import and export, allowing you or an artist to create assets for your project. See Figure 2-13.

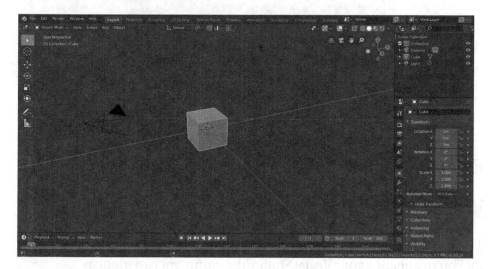

Figure 2-13. *Blender 2.8*

Gimp (Windows, macOS, Linux)

Gimp (`www.gimp.org/`), version 2.10.12 at the time of this writing, offers an easy-to-use open source image editor. In addition, being cross-platform Gimp supports all of the major file formats for both import and export. See Figure 2-14.

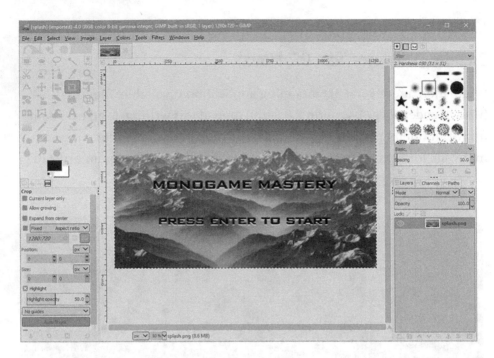

Figure 2-14. *Gimp 2.10.12*

Visual Studio Extensions

The following are a few highly recommended free Visual Studio extensions for you to enhance your Visual Studio/development experience.

Live Share (2019 and Code)

In a multiple-person development team, getting live help or a live code review can be challenging. Fortunately, a free extension called Live Share (https://marketplace.visualstudio.com/items?itemName=MS-vsliveshare.vsls-vs) offers this functionality and is highly beneficial for distributed teams where in-person meetups are difficult or impossible. See Figure 2-15.

Figure 2-15. *Visual Studio Live Share*

Visual Studio Spell Checker (2019)

On a large project, you will often have an extensive amount of strings, variables, and comments. More than likely, you will also have spelling errors scattered throughout your code. As a result, I strongly suggest installing the Visual Studio Spell Checker extension (`https://marketplace.visualstudio.com/items?itemName=EWoodruff.VisualStudioSpellCheckerVS2017andLater&ssr=false#overview`).

Visual Studio IntelliCode (2019 and Code)

With the advent of machine learning becoming an integral part of the technology industry, Microsoft has provided a machine learning code analysis extension that builds a custom model based on your code. When working with a distributed team or just as an additional consistency check, I strongly suggest installing this extension (`https://marketplace.visualstudio.com/items?itemName=VisualStudioExptTeam.VSIntelliCode`) and creating a model (just a single click). See Figure 2-16.

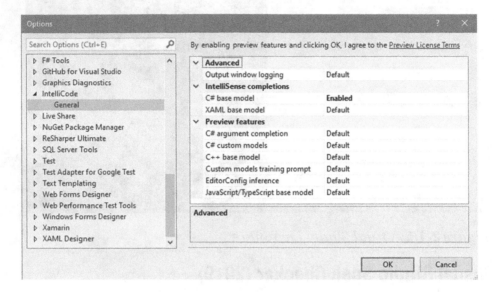

Figure 2-16. *Visual Studio IntelliCode*

Summary

In this chapter, you learned how to configure your development for MonoGame development. In addition, we reviewed additional tools and Visual Studio extensions that can help your future developments.

Up next is deep diving into the MonoGame architecture.

CHAPTER 3

MonoGame Architecture

With the introduction of MonoGame and your development environment configuration behind us, we are now ready to deep dive into MonoGame's architecture. Understanding the architecture in detail will help you to understand not only future chapters but enable you to extend MonoGame as you develop your skills.

In this chapter, you will

- Learn about the MonoGame Pipeline app

- Learn about MonoGame's Game Class

- Render your first pixels in MonoGame

MonoGame Architecture

Pipeline App

When thinking about a game, some of the biggest components are the assets such as textures, music, sprites, and sound effects. MonoGame makes this extremely easy, fortunately. At the heart of MonoGame's asset pipeline is the MonoGame Pipeline app, a tool that takes game assets like texture images, sound files, or text fonts and transforms them into binary

© Jarred Capellman, Louis Salin 2020
J. Capellman and L. Salin, *MonoGame Mastery*,
https://doi.org/10.1007/978-1-4842-6309-9_3

files that can be consumed easily by the game. In addition, the asset pipeline enables the game programmer to easily reference their game assets in the code.

For those with XNA experience, building and compiling game assets was part of the build process and caused extremely long build times for almost every project. Thankfully, MonoGame allows you to use the asset pipeline app to compile the assets into a MGCB (MonoGame Content Binary) file independently from compiling the game code in Visual Studio. That way, any code change does not force your assets to be rebuilt as well.

Figure 3-1 illustrates the MonoGame Pipeline app.

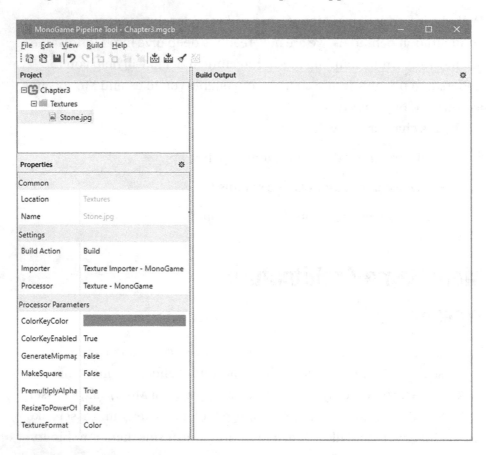

Figure 3-1. *MonoGame Pipeline app*

The assets that the pipeline tool supports out of the box are

- Effects (or shaders), which are small programs that are meant to run on your graphics card and serve to change the color of existing pixels on the screen

- 3D models in the .fbx, .X, or Open Asset Import Library formats

- Fonts, to allow the game developer to draw text on the screen

- Video files in the H.264 or .wmv formats

- Audio files in the .mp3, .ogg, .wav, or .wma formats

- Texture files

- XML files

When adding assets to the pipeline tool, an importer and processor must be selected to inform MonoGame how to process the asset. Those processors and importers are classes within the MonoGame code base that know how to read the contents of the file, how to serialize that content to a binary format, and how to transform that content into a data structure that can be used within a game's code base. In Figure 3-1, an image in the PNG format is being added to the asset pipeline and set up to be imported using MonoGame's default Texture Importer, and processed using MonoGame's default Texture processor. Doing things this way allows developers to later access the texture in the code by using something that will look like this:

```
contentManager.Load<Texture2D>("Stone");
```

For asset types not supported by the asset pipeline, MonoGame allows developers to create their own, custom importers and processors.

Generally, for all of your noncode assets, you will manually add the files in this application and rebuild your assets. In the case of textures as shown in Figure 3-1, the application will also compress, resize, and generate mipmaps for you, which are a collection of images at different resolutions. Chapter 5 will go into how to use this application in more detail for our purposes.

Game Class

At the heart of MonoGame's Framework is the Game class, which is the entry point into a game. Its main utility is to set up the game's window, with a graphics device used to draw to the screen, and to set up the important game loop. The game loop is at the heart of all video games in the wild. It is essentially an infinite loop that continuously calls the game code responsible for updating the state of the game and the code that draws things on the screen via methods that are called Update() and Draw().

The game loop must be fast and efficient. Just like a cartoon, where animation frames must be displayed at 24 frames per second to achieve the illusion of movement, a video game must appear smooth and react quickly to the player's commands. Most games try to achieve 60 frames per seconds, which means each call to both Update() and Draw() within one iteration of the game loop must take at most 1/60th of a second. When things are faster than this, MonoGame will pause to ensure that it took exactly 1/60th of a second to run through the loop and ensure a consistent output to the screen. When things are slower than this, MonoGame will try to skip the Draw() method a few times to allow the updates to catch up, which can cause the game to stutter a little. It could also drop to a lower frame rate automatically.

To create a game, we must create our own game class, which will inherit from MonoGame's Game class.

The Game class provides an extremely simple interface to the MonoGame Framework via four main functions as shown in Figure 3-2.

```
public class Game : IDisposable {
    protected virtual void Initialize();
    protected virtual void LoadContent();
    protected virtual void Update(GameTime time);
    protected virtual void Draw(GameTime time);
}
```

Figure 3-2. *Game class main methods*

The Initialize() method provides the entry point to initializing background threads, the graphics device, and other noncontent-related managers. The LoadContent() method provides the entry point for creating the SpriteBatch, the object that we will use to draw our game objects to the screen. It is also used to load Content from the aforementioned MGCB file.

As we discussed in our quick game loop introduction earlier, the Update() and Draw() methods are called successively within the game loop. Update() provides the entry point for handling game input, physics, and other non-graphics-related updates on the game timer. On the other hand, the Draw() method provides the entry point to handle all of the graphical rendering.

Over the course of this book, we will be adding manager classes to handle these scenarios in a dynamic and powerful way to create the book's game project and allow you to expand for your own creations.

Your First Rendered Pixels

Now that you have a basic understanding of the MonoGame architecture, it is finally time to create your first MonoGame Project in Visual Studio. Those who want the pre-setup project can look at the chapter3 folder for the Visual Studio Solution and Project and skip to the subsection, "Diving into the Project."

Creating the Solution and Project

For this step by step, I will be using Visual Studio 2019 on Windows as configured in Chapter 2. If you have not either installed and configured Visual Studio or MonoGame, please return to Chapter 2 and then come back to this section.

First, launch Visual Studio and you will be presented with the Create a new project dialog as shown in Figure 3-3. If your settings are configured to not show the Create a new project dialog on startup, simply click File ➤ New ➤ Project.

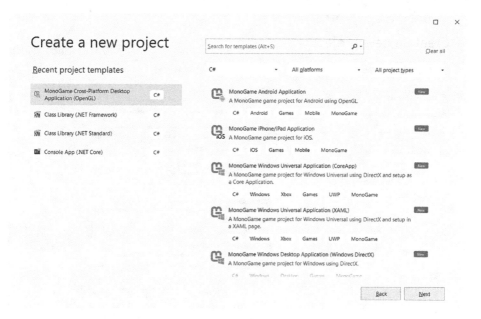

Figure 3-3. *Visual Studio 2019 Create a new project dialog*

In the Search bar at the top, type "MonoGame". If Visual Studio does not return any results, please verify you have properly installed MonoGame as detailed in Chapter 2. Otherwise, you will see many different options. MonoGame is a cross-platform library and can be used to create video games on phones, tablets, on Linux or MacOS, on Windows, and on consoles, such as the Nintendo Switch, the Xbox, or the PlayStation. But because some of these options require some platform-specific code, you must choose the project that satisfies your goals.

We will be building a PC game, so we have two classic options: a DirectX- or OpenGL-based game. While DirectX will work on Windows and Xbox, it will not work on Linux or MacOS systems. However, OpenGL is a graphical library that has been cross-platform for a long time. Select "MonoGame Cross-Platform Desktop Application (OpenGL)" and click Next, as shown in Figure 3-4.

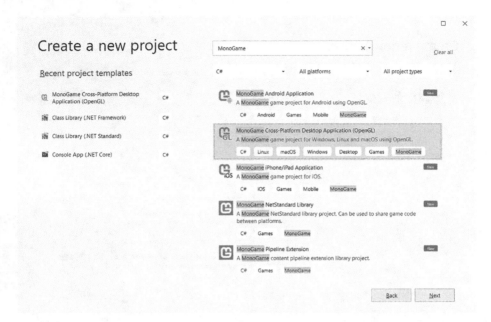

Figure 3-4. *Visual Studio 2019 Create a new project dialog with the MonoGame Cross-Platform Desktop Application (OpenGL) template selected*

On the next dialog, feel free to give the project name any name you wish; as this is Chapter 3, I have given it the name chapter3 as shown in Figure 3-5.

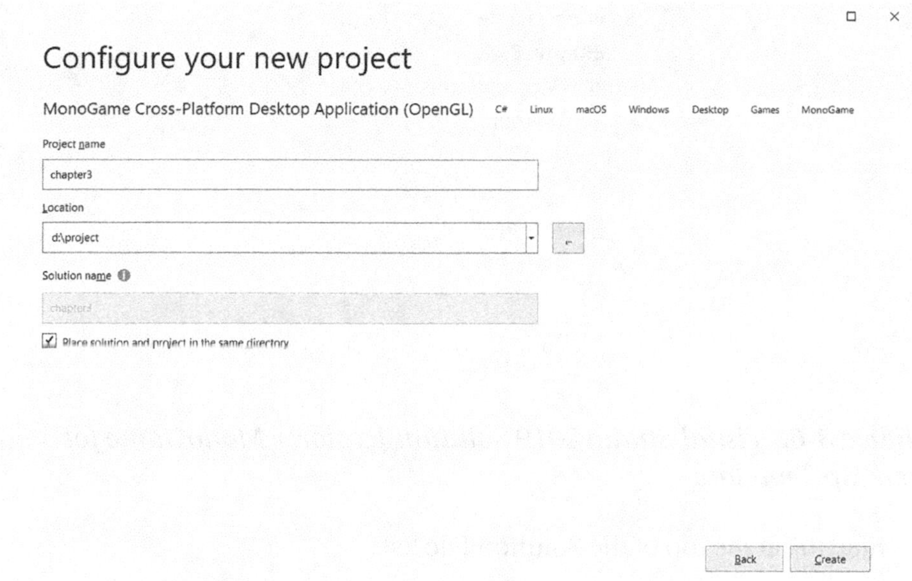

Figure 3-5. *Visual Studio 2019 Configure your new project dialog*

After entering your project name, click Create. You will then be presented with a blank canvas for MonoGame.

Diving into the Project

Now that we have the project and solution created, let us review all of the files that come in the basic MonoGame template. The exact files may vary based on the platform and future revision, but I have personally not seen much variation between versions over the years.

Let us begin by looking at the Solution Explorer (Ctrl+W,S on Windows if your configuration is defaulted to have it closed). You should see something very similar to Figure 3-6.

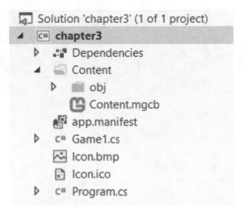

Figure 3-6. *Visual Studio 2019 Solution Explorer MonoGame for Desktop Template*

Starting at the top of the Solution File list:

- Content.mgcb: The file that contains all of your assets, such as textures, music, and sound effects, among others. In the template and for the sake of this chapter, it will remain empty.

- Game1.cs: A default extended Game class implementation that will update later in this chapter.

- Icon.ico: Icon for the project (defaulted to the MonoGame Icon)

- Program.cs: Contains the Program's Main method and call to the Game1 class

Let's update the project and rename the Game1.cs file. Right-click the file and select the "Rename" option. Rename the file to MainGame.cs. Then, build and run the project; you should see a window popup like in Figure 3-7.

Figure 3-7. *Chapter 3 example*

Diving into MainGame.cs

Open the MainGame.cs file. Starting at the top of the file, you may notice the usage of Microsoft.XNA namespaces vs. MonoGame:

```
using Microsoft.Xna.Framework;
using Microsoft.Xna.Framework.Graphics;
using Microsoft.Xna.Framework.Input;
```

The reasoning for keeping the old XNA name in place is that the abundance of documentation, samples, and existing code that would need to be updated would be a huge undertaking for an open source project. It had been discussed possibly changing it for a future major version, but nothing at the time of this writing has been put in place.

Next up in the source file is the declaration of two private variables:

```
GraphicsDeviceManager graphics;
SpriteBatch spriteBatch;
```

The GraphicsDeviceManager class provides the MonoGame interface to the graphics card. For those who have done DirectX 12 or Vulkan, this is akin to enumerating a device and having a single class object to request commands. In addition, the class also provides device information exposed in the GraphicsDevice.Adapter property. A graphics device is a low-level module that is responsible for rendering graphical objects and sending them to the screen. In the next chapter, we will dive into some of the other properties of the GraphicsDeviceManager such as requesting the video resolution, full screen or not, and multisampling.

The SpriteBatch class provides the main interface to the extremely powerful 2D Rendering Engine provided in the MonoGame Framework. While the name implies it is only used for sprites, it actually provides a rendering interface for all 2D rendering.

Next in the file is the constructor call for Game1. Change the name of the class to MainGame so it will match the name of the file:

```
public MainGame()
{
    graphics = new GraphicsDeviceManager(this);
    Content.RootDirectory = "Content";
}
```

In line 3, the graphics variable is initialized, and on line 4, the Root Directory is set to Content. Referring back to Figure 3-6, you will notice the Content.mgcb file resides in the Content subfolder. If you rename this folder, be sure to update this line. This book and all examples will retain this name.

The Initialize method is initially empty and simply calls its base class's Initialize method. Let's take a look at LoadContent:

```
protected override void LoadContent()
{
    // Create a new SpriteBatch, which can be used to draw
        textures.
    spriteBatch = new SpriteBatch(GraphicsDevice);

    // TODO: load your game content here
}
```

In line 4, the spriteBatch is initialized. Traditionally, this LoadContent method also gives us with the opportunity to load our assets from the pipeline tool, which we will do in Chapter 5.

Moving down to the next method, Update:

```
protected override void Update(GameTime gameTime)
{
    if (GamePad.GetState(PlayerIndex.One).Buttons.Back ==
    ButtonState.Pressed || Keyboard.GetState().IsKeyDown
    (Keys.Escape))
                Exit();

    // TODO: Add your update logic here

    base.Update(gameTime);
}
```

Line 3 in the preceding code block as you probably guessed checks to see if the Escape button has been hit and, if so, exits the game.

The TODO comment on line 6 earlier typically gets expanded to include calls to collision detection, AI, physics, and other non-graphics-related components in video games. This is where the state of the game is maintained, where game object coordinates in the game world are updated, where enemy game objects' movement speeds are updated based on some acceleration variable, or where verifying if the player died takes place. A lot can happen here, but we will make sure to structure our code so this method doesn't get overwhelmed with too many details and responsibilities.

Line 8 calls the Game class's Update method, which for the scope of this book we will retain as we will use the Game class for simplicity.

Last but not least is the Draw method:

```
protected override void Draw(GameTime gameTime)
{
    GraphicsDevice.Clear(Color.CornflowerBlue);

    // TODO: Add your drawing code here

    base.Draw(gameTime);
}
```

The call to the GraphicsDevice.Clear method on line 3 in the preceding code block clears the screen to CornflowerBlue. Clearing the screen before rendering new objects is important to avoid previously drawn artifacts from remaining on the screen and avoiding objects from creating trails as they move. For most of the book, we will be clearing to Black, but to demonstrate actual rendering has occurred, the default template clears to CornflowerBlue.

The TODO comment on line 5 earlier is where we will be calling our single call to render all of the objects in the next chapter.

Lastly, the call to base.Draw on line 7 calls the base Draw method of the Game class, which is important for MonoGame programmers that want to use Game Components in their code. While this won't be the case for us in this book, we recommend leaving the base call in place, just in case.

Execution Order

A common question I often ask myself when using a new framework, especially when extending or first deep diving, is in what order should the methods be called?

Using the project as a reference, here is the order:

1. Program Class ➤ Creates Game object ➤ Calls Run on the Game object

2. MainGame Constructor

3. MainGame.Initialize

4. MainGame.LoadContent

5. Game Loop ➤ (MainGame.Update and then MainGame.Draw)

6. MainGame.UnloadContent

7. MainGame.Finalizer

Knowing this order, receiving null exceptions, content issues, or other rendering anomalies may be due to doing operations out of order.

Summary

In this chapter, you learned about the MonoGame architecture and you dove into the default template and set up your first project. In addition, you ran and rendered your first pixels with the MonoGame Framework!

Up next is planning the architecture for the rest of the book with MonoGame.

CHAPTER 4

Planning Your Game Engine

Building upon the last chapter, in this chapter we will start architecting the game engine. For each chapter, we will implement another component until completion. Proper planning and architecting are crucial to creating a successful engine, game (or any program for that matter). This chapter will also go over a couple design patterns used in game engines in case you want to explore other patterns in your own projects.

In this chapter, you will learn

- Game engine design patterns

- Programming design patterns

- State management

- MonoGame architecture

Game Engine Design

Game engines are used everywhere. From simple indie games to AAA games with multimillion-dollar budgets, any time developers want to reuse common game code, an engine is created. The most sophisticated engines are highly complex pieces of code that take teams dozens (or more) of months and in some cases years to release. The Unreal Engine

3 has over two million lines of code for reference. On the other hand, we could design a very small and simple engine that simply draws game objects for us and capture player input without doing anything else. However, properly designing and architecting prior to writing any code is critical to ensuring its reusability. In this chapter, we will first dive into the major components of the game engine we will write using the MonoGame Framework. Figure 4-1 shows the overall architecture of the engine.

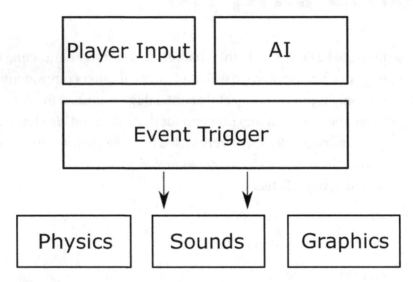

Figure 4-1. *Game engine design architecture*

Player Input

Driving many (if not most) of the interaction of your game engine is the input. Depending on your target platform, this can include everything from a standard gamepad, keyboard, and mouse combination to touch or head tracking via a virtual reality headset. In Chapter 6 we will deep dive into integrating a generic interface to gracefully handle the various inputs that exist today for games and future proofing as much as possible.

Artificial Intelligence (AI)

Artificial intelligence has been a critical component of games for decades. One of the earliest examples being *Space Invaders* in the late 1970s. While primitive by today's standards, *Space Invaders* offered the player a challenge against the computer-controlled players with two different enemy types. In today's games, pathfinding and decision trees drive most games.

Event Triggers

At the heart of our engine and many others is an Event Trigger system. The idea behind this is to define a generic event such as a Player clicks the left mouse button. The actual game would then listen in on this event and perform one or more actions. The advantage here is to keep complexity to a minimum. A more traditional programming approach here would be to have specific calls to Render the Player, but then when the player clicked the right button have very similar code in another Render the Player method. This approach as you can see also creates DRY (don't repeat yourself) violations. Later in this chapter, we will create the basis for our Event Trigger subsystem that we will build on in subsequent chapters.

Graphical Rendering

One of the most focused on components in a game engine is the graphics. Graphics rendering in most modern game engines includes sprites, 3D models, particles, and various texturing passes, to name a few. Fortunately, MonoGame provides easy-to-use interfaces, and for the purposes of this book, we will only focus on 2D rendering. Over the course of the remaining chapters, we will expand the rendering capabilities of our engine. In addition, we will specifically deep dive into adding a particle subsystem in Chapter 8.

Sound Rendering

Often overlooked, sound rendering is arguably equally critical to provide your audience with a high-quality auditory experience. Imagine watching your favorite action film without sound or music – it is missing half of the experience. In MonoGame, fortunately, it is very easy to add even a basic level to your game engine to provide both music and sound. Those that have done XNA development in the past, MonoGame has overhauled the interface and does not require the use of the XACT (Cross-Platform Audio Creation Tool). At a high level, MonoGame provides a simple Song class for as you probably inferred for music and SoundEffect for your sound effects. We will dive more into audio with MonoGame in Chapter 7 by adding music and sound effects to our engine.

Physics

Depending on the game, physics may actually be a more critical component than sound, input, or even graphics. There is a growing genre of games where the focus is on physics with relatively simple graphics such as Cut the Rope 2 or Angry Birds 2, where birds are slingshot toward precariously balanced structures that crumble to the ground as the bird crashes into its foundations. Much like the sound and graphic triggers, physics triggers may cause additional events such as the main character sprite colliding with an enemy, which in turn would cause an animation, health, and possibly the enemy to be destroyed.

State Management

State management is a common pattern to apply in games and MonoGame in particular due to the simple design it offers. The idea behind state management is that no matter how complex the video game, each screen, like the start menu that appears when the game is launched or the screen that displays the gameplay, can be broken into their own unique state.

Take, for instance, a traditional game's different states:

- Splash Screen

- Main Menu

- Gameplay

- End of Level Summary

Each of these states often offers different input schemes, music, and sounds effects, not to mention different rendering of assets.

For example, a splash screen typically is comprised of

- Full-screen scaled image or animated video

- Music

- Timed-based transitions or input-based progression

- An input manager that waits on the user to start the game by pressing some key on their input device

On the other hand, the gameplay state will bring in physics, particles, and AI agents used to control enemies. It also has a much more complex input manager, capturing player movement and actions precisely. The gameplay state could also be responsible for synching up game state over a network if the player is playing with friends on the Internet. All this to say that breaking your game into groups of similar states will help as you begin to architect your game. Akin to designing around inheritance, properly grouping similar functionality and only extending when necessary will make the time to maintain your project and the development effort much smaller.

To further illustrate, let us look at a few of the MonoGame-powered Stardew Valley's states in Figures 4-2, 4-3, and 4-4.

Figure 4-2. *Stardew Valley Main Menu*

Figure 4-3. *Stardew Valley Menus*

Figure 4-4. *Stardew Valley Gameplay*

Starting with Figure 4-2, the Stardew Valley Main Menu state is comprised of

- Layered animated sprites (some aligned)

- Clickable buttons

- Background music

While Figure 4-3's Character Creation state is comprised of those same elements with the addition of input fields and more complex positioning of elements, allowing the player to create a new character with the desired appearance.

Finally, Figure 4-4 shows the main gameplay screen and has many components of the first two states but increases the complexity of the graphical rendering by adding game objects that can change over time and allowing the player to move around the game world.

Implementing the Architecture of the Engine

Now that each of the components in a modern game engine has been reviewed, it is now time for us to begin architecting our engine.

For those wanting to download the completed solution, see the chapter-4 folder for both the blank project in the start folder and the completed project in the end folder.

Creating the Project

Following the same steps we reviewed in Chapter 3, we will be creating the same project type for this chapter. Going forward, keep in mind this chapter's project will be the basis for all remaining chapters of the book. Like in the previous chapter, create a new MonoGame Cross-Platform Desktop Application (OpenGL) project and rename the Game1.cs file and Game1 class to MainGame.cs and MainGame. After this, you should see a project like that shown in Figure 4-5.

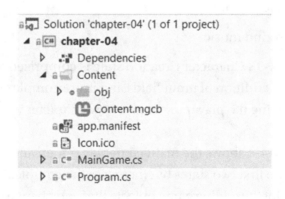

Figure 4-5. *Visual Studio 2019 showing the blank Chapter 4 project*

Creating the State Classes

As reviewed earlier in this chapter when we talked about state management, the main ideology in state management is an inheritance model to create a structure and cut down on the amount of code reuse for each state of your game. For the scope of this chapter, we will be creating the initial *BaseGameState* class followed by an empty SplashState and empty *GameplayState* class to be populated in the next chapters. Figure 4-6 illustrates the relationship between these states.

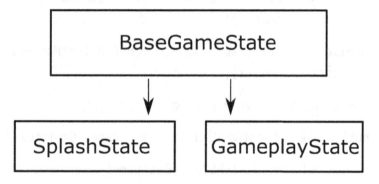

Figure 4-6. *Game States to be implemented*

You will find in the following texts the starting code for our abstract BaseGameState class, which we will build upon throughout this book. Open up the chapter-4 end solution and look at the BaseGameState.cs class in States\Base\BaseGameState.cs file:

```
using System;
using System.Collections.Generic;
using System.Linq;

using chapter_04.Objects.Base;
```

```csharp
using Microsoft.Xna.Framework.Content;
using Microsoft.Xna.Framework.Graphics;

namespace chapter_04.States.Base
{
    public abstract class BaseGameState
    {
        private readonly List<BaseGameObject> _gameObjects =
            new List<BaseGameObject>();

        public abstract void LoadContent(ContentManager
            contentManager);

        public abstract void UnloadContent(ContentManager
            contentManager);

        public abstract void HandleInput();

        public event EventHandler<BaseGameState> OnStateSwitched;

        protected void SwitchState(BaseGameState gameState)
        {
            OnStateSwitched?.Invoke(this, gameState);
        }

        protected void AddGameObject(BaseGameObject gameObject)
        {
            _gameObjects.Add(gameObject);
        }
```

```
public void Render(SpriteBatch spriteBatch)
{
    foreach (var gameObject in _gameObjects.OrderBy
        (a => a.zIndex))
    {
        gameObject.Render(spriteBatch);
    }
}
}
}
```

Let's start with the abstract method declarations of LoadContent and UnloadContent. These methods will provide an interface for, as you probably guessed, the loading and unloading of content. MonoGame uses the ContentManager class object to provide an easy-to-use interface to load content at runtime. We will cover this in detail in the next chapter when diving into asset management. For now, keep in mind that these methods will handle the state-specific unloading and loading of content.

The other abstract method, HandleInput, will provide a method for state-specific input handling. For this chapter, we will keep our implementations simple. In Chapter 6, as mentioned earlier, we will deep dive into abstracting the input handling.

The OnStateSwitched event and the SwitchState method provide both the method to switch the state from another state and the event for the main class to listen for. Any state class implementing this BaseGameState class will be able to call the SwitchState method and pass in the new state we wish to switch to. For example, pressing the Enter key in the SplashScreen state will call SwitchState and specify that we want to now use the Gameplay state. The Switch State method triggers an event that our MainGame class will respond to by unloading the current state and then loading the new state. At the next game loop iteration, the new state's Update and Draw methods will start being called.

The AddGameObject method is the state method to add objects to the List collection of BaseGameObjects, which is used to keep track of game objects we want to draw on the screen. In future chapters, we will be using this method to add sprites, static images, and other objects to this list.

Lastly, the Render method provides a single method to iterate through all the game objects we want to render on the screen. This method is called from the main Draw method in the MainGame class. It takes all the game objects in other _gameObjects list and orders them by zIndex before drawing them. A zIndex is a technique to order game objects from farthest to closest. When MonoGame draws things to the screen, every drawn object will overwrite objects that were drawn before it. While this is desirable in the cases where objects closer to the viewer must hide objects farther away, the opposite is not something we want to do. For example, clouds should be drawn in front of the sun, not behind. So when we create game objects, we must draw them in order and that's what we use the zIndex for. Why "z"? Because in 2D games we use an (X, Y) coordinate system where the X axis is horizontal and the Y axis is vertical. In 3D space, there is a third axis called Z, so we are essentially representing depth using a zIndex. Note that if every game object is at zIndex = 0, then our base state class cannot guarantee that everything will be drawn in the correct order.

Creating the Scaler and Window Management

Now that we have looked at our basic state management starting code, ahead of actually rendering anything on the screen, we need to handle scaling and supporting both windowed and full-screen modes.

Window Scaling

The idea behind window scaling is for your audience to enjoy the game as you intended regardless of the resolution. Take Figure 4-5. The window is currently set to a width of 640 and height of 480 pixels, while the texture has a width and height of 512 pixels. Given these dimensions and as shown in Figure 4-7, it consumes almost the entire screen.

Figure 4-7. *Unscaled 640x480 window with a 512x512 texture*

Common in games for the last two decades is the choice of resolution, so let us retry this same rendering at a resolution of 1024x768. Figure 4-8 depicts this.

Figure 4-8. *Unscaled 1024x768 window with a 512x512 texture*

As clearly shown, the visual experience for the higher resolution consumer of your game is significantly different.

Fortunately, MonoGame offers a very easy way to ensure this experience inconsistency is resolved. The approach assumes you design around a target resolution such as 1080p (1920x1080) if you are targeting PC or home consoles. Once the resolution has been decided, all of your assets should be produced with this resolution in mind. Images such as splash or background images should be this resolution or higher. Asset creation and management will be covered in more detail in the next chapter; however, keeping with this simple rule will help you as you start making your content.

After the target resolution has been decided, we will add a simple scale for both width and height relative to the target resolution. For instance, in the two examples, let us use 640x480 as the target resolution and keep the user resolution set to 1024x768. After implementing our scaler, see Figure 4-9. Notice outside of being larger (as expected), the experience is identical to the 640x480 screenshot in Figure 4-9.

Figure 4-9. *Scaled 1024x768 window with a 512x512 texture*

Now let us dive into the code that drove this change. First, we need to define some new variables in our MainGame class:

```
private RenderTarget2D _renderTarget;
private Rectangle _renderScaleRectangle;
```

```
private const int DESIGNED_RESOLUTION_WIDTH = 640;
private const int DESIGNED_RESOLUTION_HEIGHT = 480;

private const float DESIGNED_RESOLUTION_ASPECT_RATIO =
DESIGNED_RESOLUTION_WIDTH / (float)DESIGNED_RESOLUTION_HEIGHT;
```

The RenderTarget2D will hold the designed resolution target, while the _renderScaleRectangle variable will hold the scale rectangle. The DESIGNED* variables hold the designed for resolution; feel free to experiment with these values after adding this code.

After defining the new variables, we will need to initialize the RenderTarget and Rectangle variables to be used in our render loop in the Initialize method we had previously defined. In addition, we need to define a new method to create the rectangle in the following code:

```
protected override void Initialize()
{
    _renderTarget = new RenderTarget2D(graphics.GraphicsDevice,
        DESIGNED_RESOLUTION_WIDTH, DESIGNED_RESOLUTION_HEIGHT,
        false,
        SurfaceFormat.Color, DepthFormat.None, 0,
        RenderTargetUsage.DiscardContents);

    _renderScaleRectangle = GetScaleRectangle();

    base.Initialize();
}

private Rectangle GetScaleRectangle()
{
    var variance = 0.5;
    var actualAspectRatio = Window.ClientBounds.Width / (float)
    Window.ClientBounds.Height;

    Rectangle scaleRectangle;
```

```
if (actualAspectRatio <= DESIGNED_RESOLUTION_ASPECT_RATIO)
{
    var presentHeight = (int)(Window.ClientBounds.Width /
    DESIGNED_RESOLUTION_ASPECT_RATIO + variance);
    var barHeight = (Window.ClientBounds.Height -
    presentHeight) / 2;

    scaleRectangle = new Rectangle(0, barHeight, Window.
    ClientBounds.Width, presentHeight);
}
else
{
    var presentWidth = (int)(Window.ClientBounds.Height *
    DESIGNED_RESOLUTION_ASPECT_RATIO + variance);
    var barWidth = (Window.ClientBounds.Width -
    presentWidth) / 2;

    scaleRectangle = new Rectangle(barWidth, 0,
    presentWidth, Window.ClientBounds.Height);
}

    return scaleRectangle;
}
```

The GetScaleRectangle provides black bars akin to the scalers on your television screen based on the actual resolution vs. the design resolution. If the image being rendered to the screen is not the same size as the actual screen, the television will add black bars either horizontally or vertically to fill in the missing space. This method starts by calculating the ratio between the game window's width and height. If that ratio is lower than the designed aspect ratio, which is our desired ratio, then we need to add black bars at the top and bottom of the screen to compensate. To do so, we create a scale rectangle that goes from the (0, barHeight) coordinate and is as wide as the game window and as high as it needs to be so the whole rectangle fits onto the screen. Here, barHeight is half of the padding that is needed. Figure 4-10 shows our scale rectangle if it was displayed on the game window.

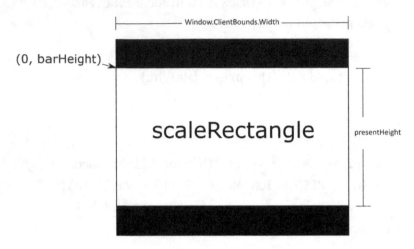

Figure 4-10. *Finding a scale rectangle that fits the game window*

Lastly, we modified the Draw method once more to render to the render target and then render the back buffer like so:

```
protected override void Draw(GameTime gameTime)
{
    // Render to the Render Target
    GraphicsDevice.SetRenderTarget(_renderTarget);

    GraphicsDevice.Clear(Color.CornflowerBlue);

    spriteBatch.Begin();

    _currentGameState.Render(spriteBatch);

    spriteBatch.End();
```

```
// Now render the scaled content
graphics.GraphicsDevice.SetRenderTarget(null);

graphics.GraphicsDevice.Clear(ClearOptions.Target, Color.
    Black, 1.0f, 0);

spriteBatch.Begin(SpriteSortMode.Immediate, BlendState.
    Opaque);

spriteBatch.Draw(_renderTarget,   renderScaleRectangle,
    Color.White);

spriteBatch.End();

base.Draw(gameTime);
}
```

A few things are happening here. First, we are setting a render target on our graphics device. This _renderTarget variable is created in the constructor like this:

```
_renderTarget = new RenderTarget2D(graphics.GraphicsDevice,
    DESIGNED_RESOLUTION_WIDTH,
    DESIGNED_RESOLUTION_HEIGHT, false,
    SurfaceFormat.Color, DepthFormat.None, 0,
    RenderTargetUsage.DiscardContents);
```

A render target is a graphical buffer used to draw things on until we are ready to send it to the screen. While we draw on the render target, nothing will happen on the screen until we decide to draw that render target. Looking at the parameters, it sets the desired game viewport resolution, the area we want to draw it. It also sets the mipmap flag to false, the background color to black (because SurfaceFormat.Color is equal to zero), and specifies that we are not using any depth stencil buffer and that our preferredMultiSampleCount is zero (this is used when doing antialiasing), and whatever we draw into our render target will not be preserved.

Then the graphics device is cleared with the blue cornflower color, which causes the screen to be painted with that same color. We are now ready for the current game state to do its thing and draw things! We are using a spriteBatch for this, which is created in the LoadContent method:

```
spriteBatch = new SpriteBatch(GraphicsDevice);
```

We briefly explained the sprite batch in Chapter 3. It is an abstraction that we will use to draw our game primitives to the screen. It is mostly used for our sprites, meaning our game textures, but it can also handle other 2D primitives like lines and rectangles. It is called a sprite batch because we will add many sprites and primitives into a single batch that will be sent to the graphics card in on single call by MonoGame. It is more efficient to build a single batch during the Draw phase of the game loop than multiple batches, although there are a few reasons why a game developer may want to build many batches in a single drawing phase. To create a new batch in our engine, we use the spriteBatch.Begin method. Then we call the Render method on the current game state and close out the sprite batch by calling spriteBatch.End.

Now that we have rendered a single frame to our render target, we are ready to draw it to the screen, which we do by setting the graphics devices' render target to null. We start by clearing the screen to a black color; then, we perform one more sprite batch phase, where we draw the render target into the scale rectangle we calculated earlier. Because the screen is initially cleared black and the render target was cleared to the cornflower blue color, if the designed resolution and the game window resolutions do not match, we will see black bars on the sides. We then end the sprite batch.

Adding this support early on in our engine design helps begin testing the engine across multiple resolutions and form factors such as a laptop screen vs. desktop monitor. Now that we have our window scaling, let us add in full-screen support to our window.

Full-Screen Support

Fortunately, in MonoGame, adding support for full screen is extremely easy. Enabling full-screen support is just one line. The following code shows how to have full screen enabled by setting graphics.IsFullScreen to true:

```
public MainGame()
{
    graphics = new GraphicsDeviceManager(this);

    graphics.PreferredBackBufferWidth = 1024;
    graphics.PreferredBackBufferHeight = 768;
    graphics.IsFullScreen = true;
    Content.RootDirectory = "Content";
}
```

Event System

The last major development in this chapter is adding the initial work on the event system. The idea behind this pattern is to have a single call and object or class listening to that particular event will do what it is programmed. This pattern will allow us over the course of the book adding all of the events to make a complete game.

For the scope of this chapter, we will add a single event, one to trigger the game to quit. To keep things strongly typed, we will define an enumeration like so:

```
public enum Events
{
    GAME_QUIT
}
```

Then in BaseGameState class, we have added a new EventHandler and method:

```
public event EventHandler<Events> OnEventNotification;

protected void NotifyEvent(Events eventType, object
    argument = null)
{
    OnEventNotification?.Invoke(this, eventType);

    foreach (var gameObject in _gameObjects)
    {
        gameObject.OnNotify(eventType);
    }
}
```

The idea behind this is we can notify the MainGame, who is listening to event notifications already, as well as any GameObjects that exist within the scope of the current game state by calling the OnNotify method that they all inherit and can override from the BaseGameObject base class:

```
public virtual void OnNotify(Events eventType) { }
```

The MainGame class will need to hook into the OnEventNotification event. Since we have already defined the SwitchGameState method, we will just need to add the event and define the implementation like so:

```
private void SwitchGameState(BaseGameState gameState)
{
    _currentGameState?.UnloadContent(Content);

    _currentGameState = gameState;

    _currentGameState.LoadContent(Content);

    _currentGameState.OnStateSwitched += CurrentGameState_
    OnStateSwitched;
    _currentGameState.OnEventNotification += _currentGameState_
    OnEventNotification;
}

private void _currentGameState_OnEventNotification(object
    sender, Enum.Events e)
{
    switch (e)
    {
        case Events.GAME_QUIT:
            Exit();
            break;
    }
}
```

With most events not needing to notify the MainGame class, this will be one of the few if any events you will need to handle specifically.

The last change we need to do is handle pressing the Enter button on the GameplayState class to trigger this event. For this, we will use code that will be explained in Chapter 6 when we discuss the different ways to capture player input. In the meantime, the following code checks if a gamepad's back button is pressed or if the keyboard's Enter key is pressed, in which case it fires the GAME_QUIT event:

```
public override void HandleInput()
{
    if (GamePad.GetState(PlayerIndex.One).Buttons.Back ==
        ButtonState.Pressed ||
        Keyboard.GetState().IsKeyDown(Keys.Enter))
    {
        NotifyEvent(Events.GAME_QUIT);
    }
}
```

Summary

In this chapter, you learned about game engine design and state management and implemented the initial architecture for the engine that will drive the project going forward.

In the next chapter, we will dive into the Asset Pipeline providing sprite loading to liven up our newly created engine.

CHAPTER 5

Asset Pipeline

Now that we have a firm understanding of the game engine architecture to be reviewed in this book, it is time to focus on the next major component of our engine: assets. As briefly discussed in Chapter 3, MonoGame provides an easy-to-use and expandable interface to accessing assets. Over the course of this chapter, we will

- Learn how the MonoGame Asset Pipeline works

- Learn how to use the MonoGame Asset Tool

- Integrate the Asset Pipeline into our engine

- Add a player sprite to the game

MonoGame Asset Pipeline

For those with XNA experience, the Asset Pipeline will be very familiar to you as MonoGame builds upon the XNA Asset Pipeline. The major change is that XNA required the assets to be compressed and packed at build time. This caused a major issue for larger projects where the build and testing times were considerable. Thankfully, MonoGame switched this to split the building of the Asset Pipeline and building of your code by providing the MonoGame Pipeline Tool (to be discussed in the next section).

© Jarred Capellman, Louis Salin 2020
J. Capellman and L. Salin, *MonoGame Mastery*,
https://doi.org/10.1007/978-1-4842-6309-9_5

In addition, MonoGame continues to provide all of the benefits that XNA's pipeline offered:

1. Extensibility to support custom file formats

2. Built-in support for XML, video, music, sound, and image

3. Image compression optimizations for each platform (DXTC, for instance, on PCs)

4. Loading system utilizing C#'s generics

The pipeline as of this writing supports asset optimizations and targeting for

1. PCs (Windows, Linux, MacOS X)

2. Consoles (Xbox 360, Xbox One, Switch, PS Vita, PSP, PS4)

3. Mobile (iOS and Android)

4. Raspberry Pi

ContentManager Class

At the core of the Asset Pipeline inside our engine that we will be continuing to evolve throughout this book is the ContentManager class. This class will provide the main interface to both load and retrieve content of various types such as sound, graphics, and levels. At a high level, the following methods are the main methods to provide this functionality. As a reminder, the source code for this class and all examples found in this book are available at www.apress.com/ISBN.

T LoadLocalized<T>(string assetName)

The LoadLocalized method as the name implies takes the assetName parameter and then builds the localized assetName in a loop like so:

```
string localizedAssetName = assetName + "." + cultureName
```

where cultureName is derived from both the CultureInfo.CurrentCulture. Name and CultureInfo.CurrentCulture.TwoLetterISOLanguageName. For example, the former would return "en-US" and the latter would return "en". For localized fonts, text graphics and audio files using the LoadLocalized should be used instead of Load.

I should note, if no localized assets are found, MonoGame automatically falls back to the Load method.

T Load<T>(string assetName)

The Load method takes a type of T and internally calls the ReadAsset method. Unfortunately, at this time there are no constraints on the type of T; therefore, I should caution the types passed in. Upon successful reading of the asset, the object is added to the internal loadedAssets dictionary based on the assetName (it is used as the key). Not commonly known, if the type of T and the assetName match a preexisting key/value pair, the call to ReadAsset is avoided and the object is simply returned.

void Unload()

The Unload method as the name implies calls the dispose method on all of the disposable assets that were previously loaded. In addition, both the loadedAssets Dictionary and disposableAlerts List collection are also cleared.

In the Game class that we have and will utilize throughout this book, the ContentManager class is accessible via the Content property.

MonoGame Pipeline Tool

Key to the pipeline is the MonoGame Pipeline Tool (depicted in Figure 5-1). This tool provides a clear separation of concerns between the code for your MonoGame project and your assets. This separation provides an easy-to-use tool for artists, audio engineers, and software engineers collaborating on larger projects. Checking in the compiled content file and assets to source control is an easy way to develop a project following the agile process.

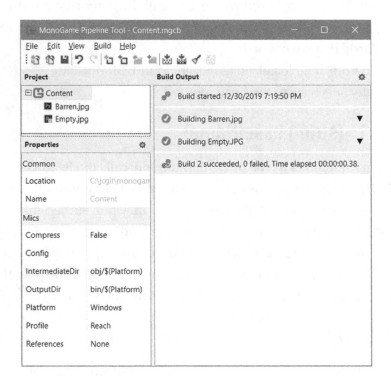

Figure 5-1. *MonoGame Pipeline Tool*

For those curious, the pipeline tool as of the 3.10 release supports MacOS X and Linux, whereas prior to that release the tool was for Windows only. The same functionality exists on all three platforms with no known differences as of this writing.

Integrate the Asset Pipeline into the Engine

Now that we have reviewed MonoGame's built-in Asset pipeline functionality, let us implement a proper way to handle asset loading and unloading in our engine.

You may recall in previous examples we simply referenced the ContentManager inside the LoadContent and UnloadContent methods in our Game States. This has the benefit of following a singleton pattern, but also doesn't provide any way to handle global assets. The reason being, when calling Unload on the ContentManager, all assets are unloaded. In a game, you more than likely have common assets such as fonts, sounds, and graphics that you wouldn't want to have to reload on every game state. You might be wondering why the ContentManager doesn't provide a way to unload certain objects – this has been discussed and requested as a feature in a future version.

To work around this limitation in the current version of MonoGame, the widely accepted solution is to simply pass in the main ContentManager and create a local copy within each Game State. For the scope of this chapter, that is the solution we will apply.

Now let us dive into the enhancements to our engine!

BaseGameState

You may recall, the abstract BaseGameState class is the primary class powering all of our game engine's states to derive from. For the scope of the chapter, we will be making several changes to support the new content loading.

The first change is to add a constant variable for the fallback texture (to be discussed in the next section):

```
private const string FallbackTexture = "Empty";
```

The second change is to add a private variable to hold the ContentManager class:

```
private ContentManager _contentManager;
```

The third change is to add a new method to initialize the private ContentManager variable:

```
public void Initialize(ContentManager contentManager)
{
    _contentManager = contentManager;
}
```

The fourth change is to swap the abstract UnloadContent method in favor of an implemented method that calls our new private ContentManager's Unload method:

```
public void UnloadContent()
{
    _contentManager.Unload();
}
```

The last change is to add a wrapper around the loading of textures along with the fallback to our fallback texture in case of a missing texture asset:

```
protected Texture2D LoadTexture(string textureName)
{
    var texture = _contentManager.Load<Texture2D>(textureName);

    return texture ?? _contentManager.Load<Texture2D>
    (FallbackTexture);
}
```

As noted in the ContentManager class deep dive, this approach to wrapping the texture loading avoids accidentally passing an incompatible type of T to the Load<T> method of the ContentManager and thereby causing an exception to be thrown.

With these changes in place, we can now shift focus to the next class changes.

MainGame

With the majority of changes occurring in the BaseGameState, there are a few changes required to the MainGame class.

The first change is to update the designed resolution to be set to 1280x720 (720p):

```
private const int DESIGNED_RESOLUTION_WIDTH = 1280;
private const int DESIGNED_RESOLUTION_HEIGHT = 720;
```

The reason for this change from the previously used resolution of 1024x768 is a true splash screen asset being loaded in the next section.

The next change is to adjust the SwitchGameState method to support the new Initialize method and not pass in the ContentManager to the LoadContent method:

```
private void SwitchGameState(BaseGameState gameState)
{
    _currentGameState?.UnloadContent();

    _currentGameState = gameState;

    _currentGameState.Initialize(Content);

    _currentGameState.LoadContent();
```

```
_currentGameState.OnStateSwitched += CurrentGameState_
    OnStateSwitched;
_currentGameState.OnEventNotification += _currentGameState_
    OnEventNotification;
}
```

With these changes, the engine now provides a clear method to load a texture and proper clearing of content as game states change. The changes and new assets to complete this work are discussed in the next section. In future chapters, we will expand this functionality to include audio, fonts, and XML files.

Add a Player Sprite to the Game

Now that the engine has been updated to support texture loading, we will only need to make a few small adjustments to our game code. Remember, you can access the source code by going to www.apress.com/ISBN.

As in previous chapters, there are three components in the chapter-05 directories:

1. assets

2. start

3. end

The assets folder contains both the Adobe Photoshop (PSD) and PNG files for the new splash screen, the sample texture, and the new fighter sprite. These files have been provided for use in this chapter and for future use in other projects.

The start folder contains the code prior to any changes made in this chapter for you to follow along. Conversely, the end folder contains the completed code if you wish to simply refer back to the chapter.

Reviewing the New Assets

To demonstrate the new texture loading functionality, three new assets have been added to the solution.

The first is a true splash screen image as opposed to simply using the land texture used previously. This splash screen was rendered to 1280x720 (depicted in Figure 5-2).

Figure 5-2. *Splash screen asset*

This image will act as the image in our SplashState class.

The second asset is an empty graphic to be utilized if a particular texture asset is not found or an error occurs during load (depicted in Figure 5-3).

Figure 5-3. *Fallback texture*

This approach will make it easy to see quickly if an asset fails to load. In your future projects, I strongly suggest either using this graphic or something not used anywhere else in your project to call out that an error occurred when testing.

The last asset is our fighter plane sprite depicted in Figure 5-4.

Figure 5-4. *Player sprite*

This will be used as our player sprite in future chapters and, as you might have seen, contains transparency which MonoGame will automatically pick up during the Asset Pipeline.

84

Adding the New Assets to Our Content

To add these new assets, double-click Content.mgcb from within Visual Studio as we have done previously. If the file opens as an XML file like that in Figure 5-5, follow the following steps.

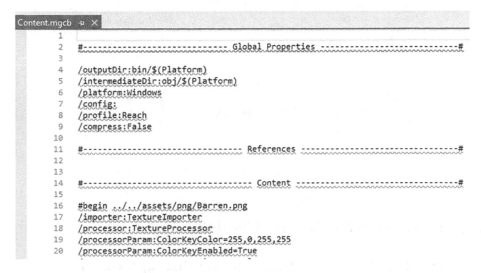

Figure 5-5. *Content.mgcb opened incorrectly as an XML file*

Step 1 is to right-click the Content.mgcb like so in Figure 5-6 and click Open With....

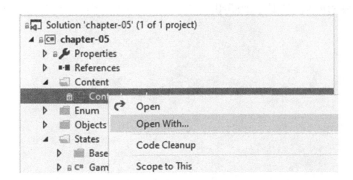

Figure 5-6. *Visual Studio Context Menu on Content.mgcb*

Once the window is opened, you will be presented with a dialog. Your view might include other options not listed; the option you are looking for is MonoGame Pipeline Tool as highlighted in Figure 5-7.

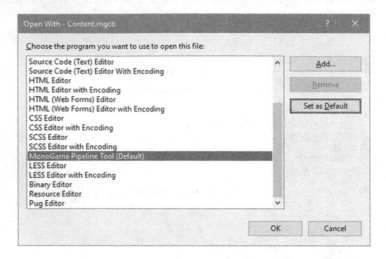

Figure 5-7. *Visual Studio Open With dialog*

Once selected, click Set as Default (to avoid having this occur again) and then click OK. After clicking OK, the MonoGame Pipeline Tool will open.

When adding content like in previous chapters, be sure when prompted to select "Add a link to the file" instead of "Copy the file to the directory" as shown in Figure 5-8.

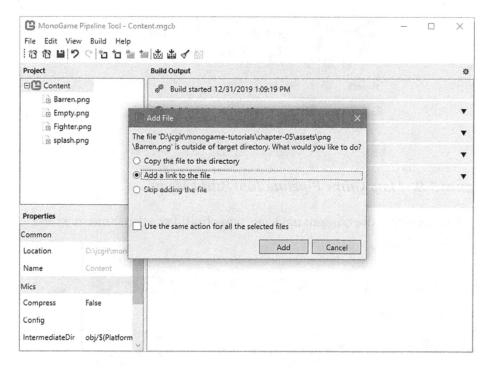

Figure 5-8. *MonoGame Pipeline Tool Add File dialog*

By clicking the "Add a link to the file" option, we will avoid having duplicate content locations. When working on a multiperson team or simply wanting one source of truth, this process avoids unnecessary churn forgetting to update multiple locations.

After adding the Empty, Fighter, and Splash assets, be sure to click Build ➤ Build, or hit the F6 key as noted in Figure 5-9.

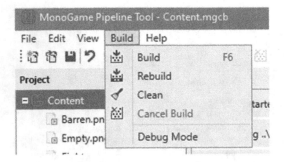

Figure 5-9. *MonoGame Pipeline Tool Build Menu*

After building the content package, you should see the same message as in Figure 5-10.

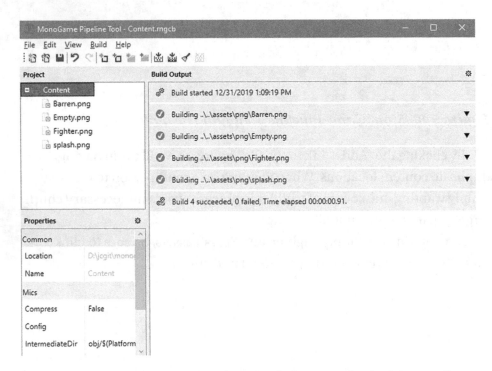

Figure 5-10. *MonoGame Pipeline Tool showing the build completes*

Game Code Changes

With the changes to our engine completed in the previous section, there are only a handful of changes required to change in our game code.

SplashState

The SplashState class as you might recall is the state that launches when our game launches. In future chapters, we will expand the functionality to include transition effects and music.

For the scope of this chapter, there are three changes required. If the following code is not clear, please refer back to Chapter 4 or follow along with the included complete source code for this chapter.

The first change is the removal of the UnloadContent method with the engine handling the unloading of content automatically inside the BaseGameState class. This removal will simplify and reduce the duplicated code as we continue to add more game states (following the don't repeat yourself mantra).

The second change is in the LoadContent method. Previously, we were using the MonoGame ContentManager class directly to load a texture. As reviewed earlier in this chapter, the LoadTexture method provides an abstraction between MonoGame and our engine. There are several reasons for this, but a few include better handling of changes to MonoGame (i.e., if the syntax changes for how to load a texture, it can be handled in one location vs. all throughout your code) in addition to extensibility within your own code.

With the changes made to the engine, we can now simply call LoadTexture like so:

```
public override void LoadContent()
{
    AddGameObject(new SplashImage(LoadTexture("splash")));
}
```

The last change is in the HandleInput method. Previously, this method looked for any key press. Keeping with the theme of making the Splash State a true splash screen, the method now looks only for the Enter key being pressed. The code behind the new method:

```
public override void HandleInput()
{
    var state = Keyboard.GetState();

    if (state.IsKeyDown(Keys.Enter))
    {
        SwitchState(new GameplayState());
    }
}
```

GameplayState

The GameplayState class as you might recall is the state that will hold our main gameplay as we progress through the chapters.

For the scope of this chapter, four changes are required.

The first change is the addition of declaring our textures as constant variables to avoid magic strings in our code:

```
private const string PlayerFighter = "fighter";

private const string BackgroundTexture = "Barren";
```

In future chapters, we will convert these constants to utilizing JSON files to create more flexibility and avoid having to hard-code textures.

The second change, like in the SplashState class, is the removal of the UnloadContent method since it is being handled inside the base class.

The third change to be made is the loading of both our sample ground texture and the fighter sprite we reviewed in the previous section. We can achieve this functionality like so:

```
public override void LoadContent()
{
    AddGameObject(new SplashImage(LoadTexture(BackgroundTexture)));
    AddGameObject(new PlayerSprite(LoadTexture(PlayerFighter)));
}
```

The last change is to switch the keyboard input to only listen for the Escape key being hit like so:

```
public override void HandleInput()
{
    var state = Keyboard.GetState();

    if (state.IsKeyDown(Keys.Escape))
    {
        NotifyEvent(Events.GAME_QUIT);
    }
}
```

In the next chapter, we will overhaul this to not be tied specifically to just keyboard input; however, for now we are mapped to only the keyboard.

Running the Application

Now that the code changes have been made, simply running the application should show the splash screen as depicted in Figure 5-11.

Figure 5-11. *Chapter 5 example showing the splash screen*

After hitting Enter, you should be presented with the ground texture and our player's fighter sprite as shown in Figure 5-12.

Figure 5-12. *Chapter 5 example showing the player sprite overlaid on top of the barren sprite*

To exit, tap the Escape key on your keyboard or click the X to close the window.

Summary

In this chapter, you learned about the MonoGame Asset Pipeline. We also dove into integrating the Asset Pipeline into our engine to support textures and creating an approach that we will use in the coming chapters to quickly add audio and video support. Lastly, we demonstrated how to use our new functionality to load a splash image in addition to our player sprite into our evolving game engine.

In the next chapter, we will dive into the handling of input in our game engine by adding support for touch, keyboard, mouse, and controller types of input.

CHAPTER 6

Input

It wouldn't be a video game without the ability for players to manipulate the state of the game in some way. We are now ready to look into taking inputs from three different sources, namely, a keyboard, a mouse, or a gamepad, and mapping that input to actions that will change the state of the game, like moving the player around the screen and shooting bullets. When we are done with this chapter, you will have a game that looks like Figure 6-1. We promise the bullets look better when they move.

Figure 6-1. *Final result*

© Jarred Capellman, Louis Salin 2020
J. Capellman and L. Salin, *MonoGame Mastery*,
https://doi.org/10.1007/978-1-4842-6309-9_6

In this chapter, you will

- Implement a scrolling background

- Learn how to manipulate the player sprite using the keyboard

- Build a generic input engine

- Learn how to use other input sources using MonoGame

Discussing the Various Input Mechanisms

MonoGame supports almost all of the user input mechanisms used by players worldwide. Whether you are a PC gamer using a keyboard and a mouse, a console player using a gamepad, or someone who likes to play on touch-enabled devices such as smartphones, MonoGame has you covered out of the box. When a player presses a button on their keyboard or gamepad, MonoGame keeps track of that particular input device's state. Our game simply needs to query that state regularly to react to what the player is trying to accomplish.

To follow along, open up the chapter-06 solution cloned from `https://github.com/Apress/monogame-mastery`. The chapter-06 directory contains two solutions: start and end. Since we are at the start of this chapter, let's open up the start solution.

Keyboard State

We briefly discussed keyboard input at the end of Chapter 5. Our two game state classes, SplashState and GameplayState, both implement a HandleInput() function that is continuously called by the MainGame class. The purpose of this function is to monitor our input devices and react to what the player is doing. Let's review the part of the GameplayState class that is of interest to us at the moment. We have hidden some of the code for brevity, but the chapter-06 end solution will have all the code.

```
using Microsoft.Xna.Framework.Input;

public class GameplayState : BaseGameState
{
    public override void HandleInput()
    {
        var state = Keyboard.GetState();

        if (state.IsKeyDown(Keys.Escape))
        {
            NotifyEvent(Events.GAME_QUIT);
        }
    }
}
```

Keyboard support in MonoGame is straightforward. Most keys are either pressed down or released, with a few exceptions to this rule for keys that toggle on and off, like Num Lock and Caps Lock. In the preceding code, we start by asking the Keyboard class for its current state. Then, we ask that state for information that is pertinent for our game. Right now, we only want to give the player a way to quit the game using the Escape key. Is the Escape key pressed at the moment? This is what the state IsKeyDown(Keys.Escape) is asking. If so, we fire the GAME_QUIT event and the MainGame class will respond by telling our program to exit.

What are the keys we can monitor? There are too many to efficiently list in the book. However, we can use Visual Studio 2019 to inspect the available options using IntelliSense or by inspecting the MonoGame library metadata.

Delete the Escape word from Keys.Escape and press Ctrl+Enter to trigger IntelliSense to pop up. You should see something like the image in Figure 6-2, and scrolling through the options should give you an indication of the wide variety of keys that can be monitored.

Figure 6-2. *IntelliSense options for the Keys enum*

Another way to see options is to inspect the MonoGame library metadata directly. We prefer this approach when exploring what functionality a library exposes to us. Let's go explore what's in Microsoft. Xna.Framework.Input.

On the Solution Explorer panel, expand the References list by clicking the arrow to its left. Figure 6-3 shows us that MonoGame.Framework is a reference that we added to our project.

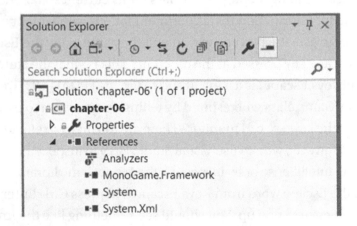

Figure 6-3. *List of references used in our game*

We can now inspect it by double-clicking the MonoGame.Framework reference. This will open the Object Browser in a new tab in Visual Studio. From there, we can start exploring. Expand MonoGame.Framework and Microsoft.Xna.Framework.Input, and then click Keys. You should see something like shown in Figure 6-4.

Figure 6-4. *All the keys pressed that MonoGame can monitor*

You can now inspect all the values that are part of that Keys enum. What you can see as well is everything that MonoGame offers us for all our input needs.

Mouse State

Our game will not immediately support using a mouse during gameplay, but we might need to use a mouse to point and click around menus. Most video games use menus to let the player configure the sound or graphics or to offer the player to resume the game or quit.

Normally, the mouse cursor is hidden from the viewport while the game is running. This can be changed by adding this line to the MainGame's Initialize() function:

```
this.IsMouseVisible = true;
```

However, even when the mouse cursor is hidden, the mouse state can still be used to monitor how a player is using their mouse. We can look at the state of the left, middle, and right buttons. We can also monitor the X and Y coordinates of the mouse and changes in the scroll wheel since the game started, which could be useful for implementing a camera zoom functionality.

If we wanted to let the player shoot bullets when pressing the left mouse button, we'd use this code:

```
var mouseState = Mouse.GetState();

if (mouseState.LeftButton == ButtonState.Pressed)
{
    // Perform shooting action!
}
```

Accessing the X and Y coordinates of the mouse is done using the following:

```
var mouseState = Mouse.GetState();

var x = mouseState.Position.X;
var y = mouseState.Position.Y;
```

Note that this will give you an X and Y coordinate based on the (0, 0) origin of the viewport, located at the top left of the game view window, just below the title bar.

Gamepad State

The gamepad is an incredibly useful gaming device. Not only is it the main device used on gaming consoles in living rooms across the world, but players also sometimes elect to use it on their computer. Monitoring the state of a gamepad is no more difficult than what we've learned so far. There are a few buttons that can be pressed and the left or right thumbstick state is represented using a 2D vector with X and Y values that are between -1 and 1, where the value zero for both coordinates indicates that the thumbstick is completely at rest, perfectly centered.

Thumbsticks also have a deadzone, which is a small area around its center that does not register any movement (Figure 6-5). This deadzone solves two problems. First, players resting their thumbs on a thumbstick can still cause it to move or jitter but they do not intend to cause their characters on the screen to move around. The deadzone ensures that this jitter remains unnoticed by the game. Second, gamepads wear out over time and thumbstick's centers can be slightly off from the (0, 0) position. The deadzone in this case prevents the game from noticing any movement. Without it, a player's character would move even when no one is touching the thumbstick.

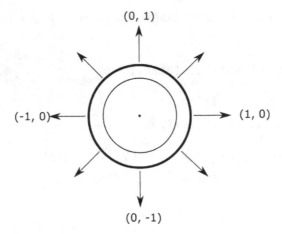

Figure 6-5. *The thumbstick's X and Y values in the (x, y) format*

To move the player using the thumbstick, you would need two things:

- The player speed

- The X and Y values from the thumbstick

When the thumbstick is pushed all the way to the left, we would register an X value of -1 and a Y value of 0. If the thumbstick was instead halfway to the left, the X value would be 0.5 instead.

The code to monitor thumbstick input would look like this:

```
var gamepadState = GamePad.GetState(PlayerIndex.One);
var newPlayerPosition = new Point(
    oldPlayerPosition.X + (gamepadState.ThumbSticks.Left.X *
    playerSpeed),
    oldPlayerPosition.Y + (gamepadState.ThumbSticks.Left.Y *
    playerSpeed)
);
```

So, if the left thumbstick was completely to the left, the X should be -1 and the Y should be 0, thus moving the character by reducing its old position by the playerSpeed value and without changing its Y position at all.

We also need to specify for which gamepad we want to get the state. Most video game consoles allow for up to four players. In this example, we were interested in what player 1 was up to.

Now that we've looked at how various inputs work in MonoGame, we are ready to add some code of our own! Our game will let the player manipulate an aircraft using the arrow keys on the keyboard and shoot down enemies using the spacebar. But before we get to this, we need one more element in our game: a scrolling background.

Scrolling Background

We all know how side scrollers work. Games like *Super Mario Bros*, where the character can only move sideways to the left or to the right and the background "scrolls" as the character, always located in the middle of the screen, "moves" around. In fact, the character is fixed in place. It is the background that moves and provides the illusion of movement.

How do the game developers achieve this illusion? They do it by moving background blocks on the screen and keeping the character in the center.

The game is filled with background blocks that overfill the viewport. When the player wants to move the character to the right, we instead take all the background blocks and move them toward the left. If there was no background block out of view, we would notice a gap created on the right edge of the screen. But since we have a background block in that area, it immediately moves in to fill in that gap. As the player keeps moving the character to the right, the leftmost background block is eventually completely offscreen. At that moment, the game will update the position of that block, so it becomes located at the right of the viewport, ready to scroll into view. Moving the character to the left would instead trigger the reverse process. Figures 6-6 and 6-7 show that process as it happens.

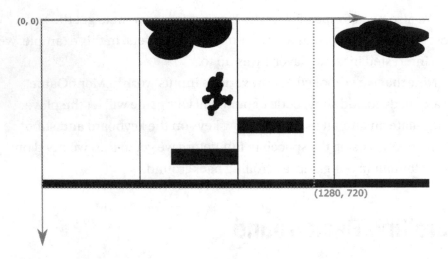

Figure 6-6. *Background blocks overfill the viewport, represented with a dotted line*

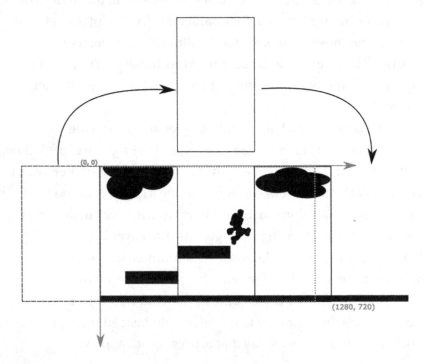

Figure 6-7. *Our character appears to be moving to the right*

104

Our game will work in a similar way, since we need to provide the illusion that our fighter jet is moving forward, in the up direction, we will instead work on making the background move downward.

Our first step is to fill up the viewport with our background terrain tile and to add an extra row of tiles just above the viewport, so they are ready to scroll down into view (Figure 6-8). Our background texture has been designed to provide seamless continuity when tiled on all sides. As the game runs and the _position.Y value increases and moves away from the origin, the tiles will move downward, causing the tiles that were offscreen at the beginning are scrolling into view (Figure 6-9). Eventually, the top tile row will be fully visible at the top of the viewport and the background will reset to its original Y position; the scrolling will then resume and create the illusion of an infinite terrain (Figure 6-10).

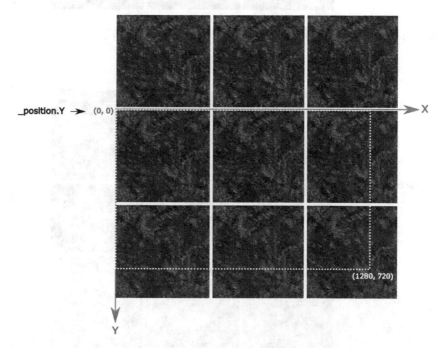

Figure 6-8. *Our tiled background. Blanks are left between the tiles to illustrate how it looks like a grid. In the game, the tiles will touch each other, and no space will be left behind*

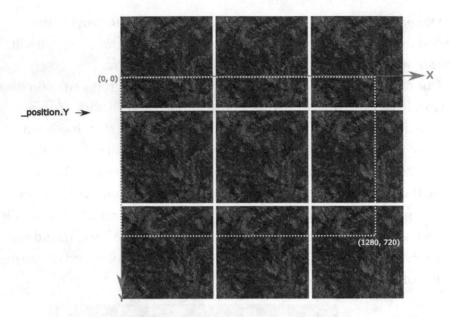

Figure 6-9. *The background appears to scroll down*

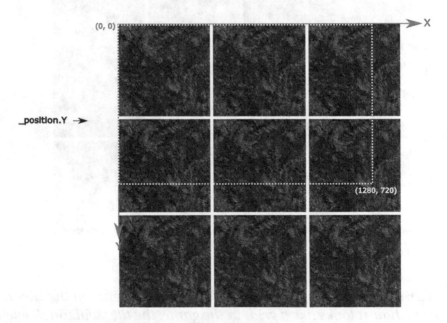

Figure 6-10. *The end of our scrolling system*

Let's create a new class called TerrainBackground and let it inherit BaseGameObject. Just like other base game objects, it should be instantiated with an existing texture and a position, which we set at (0, 0), with the goal of moving this position down along the Y axis to make it scroll.

```
public class TerrainBackground : BaseGameObject
{
    private float SCROLLING_SPEED = 2.0f;

    public TerrainBackground(Texture2D texture)
    {
        _texture = texture;
        _position = new Vector2(0, 0);
    }
}
```

Remember that _texture and _position are protected variables on the BaseGameObject parent class, which means that they are available to us inside the TerrainBackground code and in this case we are initializing _texture to the incoming parameter and making sure _position is set at the origin coordinates of (0, 0).

Drawing the background will be a little more complicated than what the BaseGameObject's Render() method does. Instead of simply drawing the object's texture at a single position, we must fill the viewport with the texture and also draw a row of terrain above the screen. To do so, we'll use a different version of the SpritBatch.Draw function that the base class uses.

For reference, this is what the base class's rendering function looks like:

```
public virtual void Render(SpriteBatch spriteBatch)
{
    spriteBatch.Draw(_texture, _position, Color.White);
}
```

The draw function has many overloads and accepts many different kinds of parameters. Here it limits itself to drawing a specific texture at a specific position that we specified when instantiating our game object. The Color.White parameter is a color mask that doesn't really concern us at the moment, except that a White mask indicates to MonoGame to render the texture as is.

However, we are going to use a different overloaded Draw function:

```
spriteBatch.Draw(_texture, destinationRectangle,
    sourceRectangle, Color.White);
```

We tell the sprite batch here to draw a certain rectangle of our texture to a certain rectangle of the viewport using a white color mask. Specifying the source rectangle is useful when a source texture contains many sprites on the same texture, which is usually the case for games with sprite animations where all animation frames of a game object, like a character bobbing up and down as it stands idle, are arranged in a grid in a single file.

When we specify a destination rectangle of a different size than the source rectangle, MonoGame will stretch or compress the image to fit. However, in our case, both rectangles will be the same size and we will use the entire terrain texture.

Our source and destination rectangles are thus defined like this:

```
var sourceRectangle = new Rectangle(0, 0, _texture.Width, _
    texture.Height);
var destinationRectangle = new Rectangle(x, y, _texture.Width,
    _texture.Height);
spriteBatch.Draw(_texture, destinationRectangle,
    sourceRectangle, Color.White);
```

As you can see, it has the same width and height as our game object texture and is positioned at an x and y coordinates that mark the location of each terrain block on our grid, computed on the Y axis from -_texture.

Height to the height of the viewport and from 0 to the width of the viewport for the X axis. The reason we start at -_texture.Height on the Y axis is to create that extra row of terrain that will scroll down into view.

Let's fill our texture blocks:

```
public override void Render(SpriteBatch spriteBatch)
{
    var viewport = spriteBatch.GraphicsDevice.Viewport;

    var sourceRectangle = new Rectangle(0, 0, _texture.Width,
    _texture.Height);

    for (int nbVertical = -1;
         nbVertical < viewport.Height / _texture.Height + 1;
         nbVertical++)
    {
        var y = (int) _position.Y + nbVertical *
            _texture.Height;
        for (int nbHorizontal = 0;
             nbHorizontal < viewport.Width / _texture.Width + 1;
             nbHorizontal++)
        {
            var x = (int) _position.X + nbHorizontal *
                _texture.Width;
            var destRectangle = new Rectangle(x, y,
                _texture.Width, _texture.Height);
            spriteBatch.Draw(_texture, destRectangle,
                sourceRectangle, Color.White);
        }
    }

    _position.Y = (int)(_position.Y + SCROLLING_SPEED) %
        _texture.Height;
}
```

109

We loop over the Y axis first and compute the y position of all our texture blocks. We know how many vertical blocks to draw by dividing the height of the viewport by the height of our texture. The outer loop is designed to go from -1 to the total number of blocks needed to accommodate the extra row we need to draw offscreen. Multiplying that number by the height of the texture, we get the exact Y coordinate where a row of texture blocks needs to be drawn. But there's a twist... we add the game object's _position.Y value to the total. That position is initialized to 0, but as the game runs, it will increase and that will cause all the rows to be drawn lower every pass through the Render() function.

Now that we know the Y coordinate of our row, we need to find the X coordinate. Similarly, we know how many texture blocks are needed by dividing the viewport width by the texture width. The inner for loop is designed to go from 0 to the total number of blocks needed to fill the screen. We then multiply that number by the texture width and add the game object's _position.X (which will always be zero at the moment, but we never know if that will change in the future) and we get each block's X coordinate.

Armed with the x and y coordinates, we can now compute our rectangles and fill the screen with blocks. When all this is done, we increment _position.Y by SCROLLING_SPEED, which will cause the background to shift down on the screen on the next rendering pass. But here is another twist... There is no need to scroll down more than one texture's width. When we reach that point, we use the modulo operator to reset the _position.Y value, causing the animation to restart from the beginning.

Okay, we got a lot done and now we are ready to replace our old terrain game object with an actual TerrainBackground object. Open up the GameplayState class, and replace this line in the LoadContent() method

```
AddGameObject(new SplashImage(LoadTexture(BackgroundTexture)));
```

with this line

```
AddGameObject(new TerrainBackground(LoadTexture(Background
Texture)));
```

This will use our new TerrainBackground class and it will automatically scroll forever.

Finally, we need to position our fighter at the bottom of this screen, right in the middle. Change the part of LoadContent() that deals with adding our fighter game object with the following code:

```
_playerSprite = new PlayerSprite(LoadTexture(PlayerFighter));
var playerXPos = _viewportWidth / 2 - _playerSprite.Width / 2;
var playerYPos = _viewportHeight - _playerSprite.Height - 30;
_playerSprite.Position = new Vector2(playerXPos, playerYPos);
```

This code as is will not compile because we have not yet modified the BaseGameState class to keep a reference to the viewport dimensions used earlier. Instead, replace the _viewportWidth and _viewportHeight by 1280 and 720, respectively, or look at the code supplied at the end of the chapter for the complete solution.

We have now located the fighter 30 pixels above the bottom of the viewport, right in the middle of the screen, and we are finally ready to start working on our generic input manager.

Creating a Generic Input Manager

The goal of our input manager is to handle our player's inputs as much as possible in a set of classes that can be reused in other games with minimal changes to make them work out of the box. We chose a pattern where the game takes in inputs from the keyboard, the mouse, or gamepads and transforms the input into commands that the game can compute. Each of our game state classes, like the GameplayState class, will only handle incoming commands instead of dealing with the input directly. See Figure 6-11.

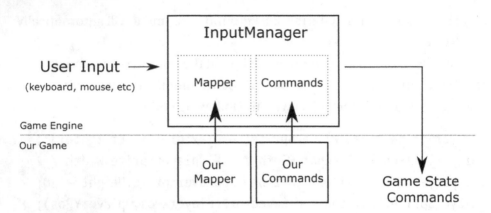

Figure 6-11. *Our game will extend the game engine's BaseInputMapper and BaseInputCommand classes and provide the extensions to the input manager*

For example, pressing the left arrow key on the keyboard during gameplay will generate a PlayerMoveLeft command that the game state will consume and cause the player sprite to move to the left.

Without knowing which commands are used by our game or which game state is currently in effect, the game engine will be able to correctly transform, or map, a player input into a game command. The idea is that each game state, like SplashState or the GameplayState, will provide the InputManager class in our engine with a specific Mapper class that knows how to map inputs to commands that the current state cares about.

It is worth noting at this point that we are not following the popular Command pattern. We simply chose the name "Command" to indicate a class that can be thought of as a command from the player to perform some action based on the user input.

The BaseInputCommand is an empty class, but it is used as a return type by the input manager and the BaseInputCommand classes. We will extend one mapper class and one command class per game state. Let's look at the GameplayInputCommand class:

```
public class GameplayInputCommand : BaseInputCommand
{
    public class GameExit : GameplayInputCommand { }
    public class PlayerMoveLeft : GameplayInputCommand { }
    public class PlayerMoveRight : GameplayInputCommand { }
    public class PlayerShoots : GameplayInputCommand { }
}
```

What we see here are a few inner classes that all inherit from GamePlayInputCommand that we'll use just like we use enums, with the main difference that we can constrain command types to our game states. The main benefit to this approach is that it'll be easier to reason about which commands belong to which game state. As we add more game states, like menus, option screens, minigames, and so on, it will be important to have an easy way to keep things organized. But first things first, take a look at the GamePlayInputMapper:

```
public class GameplayInputMapper : BaseInputMapper
{
    public override IEnumerable<BaseInputCommand>
    GetKeyboardState(KeyboardState state)
    {
        var commands = new List<GameplayInputCommand>();

        if (state.IsKeyDown(Keys.Escape))
        {
            commands.Add(new GameplayInputCommand.GameExit());
        }
```

```
if (state.IsKeyDown(Keys.Left))
{
    commands.Add(new GameplayInputCommand.
    PlayerMoveLeft());
}

if (state.IsKeyDown(Keys.Right))
{
    commands.Add(new GameplayInputCommand.
    PlayerMoveRight());
}

if (state.IsKeyDown(Keys.Space))
{
    commands.Add(new GameplayInputCommand.
    PlayerShoots());
}

    return commands;
    }
}
```

The preceding mapper is where we take user input from MonoGame, and for each input that we care about, we create a command that we add to a list. When the gameplay state class receives these commands, it will be able to execute on each one and manipulate the game state accordingly.

We now need to inject our mapper and commands into the input manager. Let's start by adding a reference to the input manager in the BaseGameState class

```
protected InputManager InputManager {get; set;}
```

and initialize it in the constructor (here is where we get the viewport dimensions that we discussed higher up):

```
protected abstract void SetInputManager();

public void Initialize(ContentManager contentMng, int
    viewportWidth, int viewportHeight)
{
    _contentManager = contentMng;
    _viewportHeight = viewportHeight;
    _viewportWidth = viewportWidth;

    SetInputManager();
}
```

Here the intention is for our game state classes that inherit this base class to implement the SetInputManager() function. The GameplayState class does it like this:

```
protected override void SetInputManager()
{
    InputManager = new InputManager(new GameplayInputMapper());
}
```

We can see now how the GameplayState class creates a custom-made input manager that will use our own input mapper, which happens to return gameplay commands that we can respond to. The SplashState class also creates its own input manager and has its own set of commands it responds to, which is the GameSelect command that triggers when the player presses the Enter key.

All we have left to do now is to respond to our game commands. Let's rewrite the GameplayState class's HandleInput() function.

```
public override void HandleInput()
{
    InputManager.GetCommands(cmd =>
    {
        if (cmd is GameplayInputCommand.GameExit)
        {
            NotifyEvent(Events.GAME_QUIT);
        }

        if (cmd is GameplayInputCommand.PlayerMoveLeft)
        {
            _playerSprite.MoveLeft();
        }

        if (cmd is GameplayInputCommand.PlayerMoveRight)
        {
            _playerSprite.MoveRight();
        }
    });
}
```

Try it out! You should see a scrolling background and have the ability to move the fighter to the left and to the right... even offscreen! Wait, this is not supposed to happen. We need to keep our player within the viewport! Let's add a function to block the player from going offscreen:

```
private void KeepPlayerInBounds()
{
    if (_playerSprite.Position.X < 0)
    {
```

```
    _playerSprite.Position = new Vector2(0, _playerSprite.
      Position.Y);
}

if (_playerSprite.Position.X > _viewportWidth -
_playerSprite.Width)
{
    _playerSprite.Position = new Vector2(_viewportWidth -
    _playerSprite.Width, _playerSprite.Position.Y);
}

if (_playerSprite.Position.Y < 0)
{
    _playerSprite.Position = new Vector2(_playerSprite.
    Position.X, 0);
}

if (_playerSprite.Position.Y > _viewportHeight -
_playerSprite.Height)
{
    _playerSprite.Position = new Vector2(_playerSprite.
    Position.X, _viewportHeight - _playerSprite.Height);

}
}
```

Here we check the position of the player object and reset it if it ever gets out of bounds. If the player moves too far to the left, its Position.X will become lower than zero, so we just readjust it to zero. If it moves too far to the right, the sprite will start going offscreen when its Position.X value becomes bigger than the width of the viewport minus the width of the sprite. In that case we reset that position as well. We also spend some time making sure the player cannot go up or down beyond the screen because we envision that we may want to start moving the aircraft up and down when we start adding enemies to the game.

Now let's call our function after the player moves:

```
_playerSprite.MoveLeft();
KeepPlayerInBounds();
```

and

```
_playerSprite.MoveRight();
KeepPlayerInBounds();
```

Shooting Bullets

You may have noticed in the commands we looked at so far that there was a PlayerShoots command. Indeed, our fighter would not be very interesting if it was only able to move left and right. So, let's shoot some bullets!

We have added a bullet sprite to the game pipeline. You can find it here: https://github.com/Apress/monogame-mastery/blob/master/chapter-06/assets/png/bullet.png.

Follow the steps described in previous chapters to add the bullet to the game pipeline and create a new BulletSprite class with a function allowing the bullet to move up to the top of the screen.

```
public class BulletSprite : BaseGameObject
{
    private const float BULLET_SPEED = 10.0f;

    public BulletSprite(Texture2D texture)
    {
        _texture = texture;
    }
```

```
public void MoveUp()
{
    Position = new Vector2(Position.X, Position.Y -
        BULLET_SPEED);
}
}
```

Now we need to prepare the bullet objects and shoot them when the player hits the space bar. We are going to update the LoadContent() function in the GameplayState class to load the texture, but we won't create the game object immediately. Instead, we'll add them to the game only when the player shoots them.

```
private const string BulletTexture = "bullet";
private Texture2D _bulletTexture;
private List<BulletSprite> _bulletList;
public override void LoadContent()
{
    // The rest of the code is omitted for brevity

    _bulletTexture = LoadTexture(BulletTexture);
    _bulletList = new List<BulletSprite>();
}
```

We are adding a list of bullets here for the purpose of tracking all the bullets that are going to fill the screen. We'll want eventually to see if a single bullet has hit an enemy so we need a way to inspect all our bullets in an easy way. The list fits that purpose. When bullets are created, we will add them to the list of game objects (so they get rendered by the game engine) and to our list of bullets.

We also need to track the game time because we don't want the player to be able to hold the spacebar down and fire an infinite stream of bullets. We want the game to be a little bit difficult and an easy way to do this is to slow down the rate of bullets to say… 5 per second? Here is how it's going to work: when the player shoots a volley of bullets, we'll note that the player is currently shooting and remember the current game time. If the player shoots again by keeping the spacebar down or by hitting it again too quickly, we will prevent the player from shooting if there was 0.2 seconds that elapsed since the last successful firing of bullets. So, let's update the code to keep track of the game time:

```
private bool _isShooting;
private TimeSpan _lastShotAt;
public override void HandleInput(GameTime gameTime)
{
    // ...
    if (cmd is GameplayInputCommand.PlayerShoots)
        {
            Shoot(gameTime);
        }
}

private void Shoot(GameTime gameTime)
{
    if (!_isShooting)
    {
        CreateBullets();
        _isShooting = true;
        _lastShotAt = gameTime.TotalGameTime;
    }
}
```

```
private void CreateBullets()
{
    var bulletSpriteLeft = new BulletSprite(_bulletTexture);
    var bulletSpriteRight = new BulletSprite(_bulletTexture);

    // Position bullets around the fighter's nose when they get
    // fired
    var bulletY = _playerSprite.Position.Y + 30;
    var bulletLeftX = _playerSprite.Position.X +
        _playerSprite.Width / 2 - 40;
    var bulletRightX = _playerSprite.Position.X +
        _playerSprite.Width / 2 + 10;

    bulletSpriteLeft.Position = new Vector2(bulletLeftX, bulletY);
    bulletSpriteRight.Position = new Vector2(bulletRightX,
        bulletY);

    _bulletList.Add(bulletSpriteLeft);
    _bulletList.Add(bulletSpriteRight);

    AddGameObject(bulletSpriteLeft);
    AddGameObject(bulletSpriteRight);
}
```

Now we need to make our bullets move up on their own. We'll do that by adding an Update() function that will get called from the main game loop. Let's add it in our base class first:

```
public abstract class BaseGameState
{
    public virtual void Update(GameTime gameTime) { }
}
```

Add this line to the MainGame's Update() function to call our current state class's Update() function:

```
_currentGameState.Update(gameTime);
```

Finally, let's implement the Update() function in our GameplayState class to make all the bullets in our bullet list move up:

```
public override void Update(GameTime gameTime)
{
    foreach (var bullet in _bulletList)
    {
        bullet.MoveUp();
    }

    // Can't shoot more than every 0.2 seconds. If it's been
    // longer, allow shooting again
    if (_lastShotAt != null &&
        gameTime.TotalGameTime - _lastShotAt >
            TimeSpan.FromSeconds(0.2))
    {
        _isShooting = false;
    }
}
```

Writing games is a lot of fun, but eventually there are a lot of tedious details that need to be taken care of. The code we have looked at here creates a lot of bullets that fly up the screen. The only problem is that once the bullets are offscreen, they are still being tracked and their position keeps moving up. Those bullets take up a little bit of memory, and even though computers are fast, iterating through our list of bullets dozens of times per second to update their position will eventually start slowing down the game. To prevent that from happening, we need to clean up bullets from the game after they have disappeared from the screen. After moving our bullets up, let's clean them up, in the same Update() function:

```
// Get rid of bullets that have gone out of view
var newBulletList = new List<BulletSprite>();
foreach (var bullet in _bulletList)
{
    var bulletStillOnScreen = bullet.Position.Y > -30;
    if (bulletStillOnScreen)
    {
        newBulletList.Add(bullet);
    }
    else
    {
        RemoveGameObject(bullet);
    }
}

_bulletList = newBulletList;
```

Summary

We did a lot of work in this chapter and our game is starting to look like a real game! We added a scrolling background after investigating how other games do the same thing. We also added a using input manager that is generic and reusable by simply creating lists of game commands and mapping user input to those commands. We also got a small glimpse of memory management and how we need to keep the game running smoothly.

Find the final version of the game code for this chapter here: `https://github.com/Apress/monogame-mastery/tree/master/chapter-06/end`.

Feel free to experiment. In the next chapter, we will add a music background track and sound effects when the player shoots bullets and when bullets hit enemies. Oh, that probably means we'll start adding enemies to our game too!

CHAPTER 7

Audio

A game without audio is like a salad without any dressing. It is still edible, but it will not be very enjoyable. In just the same way, while our game would be playable without music and sound effects, it will be hard for players to get immersed into it and be emotionally involved. Think of all the epic boss fights that exist in most video games. Besides the amazing boss mechanics, they all had a soundtrack that fired up the fight or flight instincts of the player.

Music in a game exists to create emotions and set the tone of a particular level or scenario, just like in movies, while sound effects are there to add a bit of realism to the game without being overbearing.

In this chapter, you will

- Refactor the engine to make it more reusable

- Create a sound manager and add it to the engine

- Add tracks and sound effect to the sound manager

- Trigger sound effects via game events

Refactoring the Engine

When we started out writing the code for this game, we were not too focused on making the engine code easy to reuse in future projects. While there has been a separation of concern and we clearly discussed which part of the code would be part of the engine code and which part would be

© Jarred Capellman, Louis Salin 2020
J. Capellman and L. Salin, *MonoGame Mastery*,
https://doi.org/10.1007/978-1-4842-6309-9_7

game specific, our files have all been collocated and mingled together. If we wanted to take the engine code from the beginning of this chapter and reuse it in another project, we would have to pick and choose which files need to be copied into the new project and that process isn't ideal.

The best-case scenario would be to have all our engine logic completely separated into a library we can import in other projects. Our game engine is not complete yet so we can delay this step a little longer until we are done writing its code. One thing we can do right now, however, is to start organizing the engine logic to separate it further from our game code.

Let's take a look at Figure 7-1 and the current organization of our code. The code we will look at and modify in this chapter is located here for those who would like to follow along: `https://github.com/Apress/monogame-mastery/tree/master/chapter-07/start`.

Figure 7-1. *Code organization at the beginning of this chapter*

So far most of our engine code has been base classes that game code can inherit and implement. However, this changed when we added the input manager in Chapter 6. As we prepare to add a sound manager, we need to think about how we can reorganize the code. One of our issues is that MainGame.cs contains very generic logic that could be part of the game engine if it were not for these lines of code:

```
protected override void LoadContent()
{
    // Create a new SpriteBatch, which can be used to draw textures.
    spriteBatch = new SpriteBatch(GraphicsDevice);

    SwitchGameState(new SplashState());
}
```

Everything in this file references engine code or MonoGame code, except for the LoadContent() function, which needs to know which GameState class it needs to run first. One problem is that it is currently hardwired to start the SplashState, which is very much a game-specific module. If you were creating another game using the same engine, chances are the SplashState would be very different.

One tenet of good software design is to have low coupling and high cohesion between code modules. There are many things that can increase coupling between classes and files. For example, in Figure 7-2 we have an object A accessing directly the internal variables of another object B that would instantly create a dependency of the calling object A on how the internal class B is implementing, making it harder in the future to change class B without causing issues in class A.

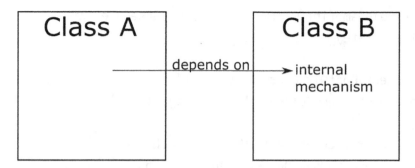

Figure 7-2. *Objects of class A depend on internal details of class B*

There will always be coupling between modules, but the goal should be to reduce the coupling between modules that belong to different areas of concern. There are fewer problems with game engine code being coupled to itself than if it was coupled to the game directly. This is where cohesion comes into the picture. Code with high cohesion within its modules and low coupling to other modules will be easier to maintain and reuse.

Let's make MainGame more generic. Instead of hard-coding our first GameState class to start with in the LoadContent() method, we will provide the class with this information via a constructor parameter. Similarly, instead of having constants within the class for the width, height, and aspect ratios of the screen resolution, we'll pass in the desired width height to the class and calculate the aspect ratio inside the constructor.

```
private int _DesignedResolutinWidth;
private int _DesignedResolutionHeight;
private float _designedResolutionAspectRatio;

private BaseGameState _firstGameState;
```

```
public MainGame(int width, int height, BaseGameState
firstGameState)
{
    Content.RootDirectory = "Content";
    graphics = new GraphicsDeviceManager(this)
    {
        PreferredBackBufferWidth = width,
        PreferredBackBufferHeight = height,
        IsFullScreen = false
    };

    _firstGameState = firstGameState;
    _DesignedResolutinWidth = width;
    _DesignedResolutionHeight = height;
    _designedResolutionAspectRatio = width / (float)height;
}
```

Now LoadContent() can use the _firstGameState variable and start the game in that state when executed:

```
protected override void LoadContent()
{
    // Create a new SpriteBatch, which can be used to draw textures.
    spriteBatch = new SpriteBatch(GraphicsDevice);

    SwitchGameState(_firstGameState);
}
```

With these changes, our MainGame.cs file now only references engine code and MonoGame code and is ready to be moved into the engine!

The responsibility to set the resolution and initial state of the game has been moved to Program.cs file, so we can set the WIDTH and HEIGHT values here and create our MainGame instance with those constants and an instance of the SplashState class:

```
private const int WIDTH = 1280;
private const int HEIGHT = 720;
static void Main()
{
    using (var game = new MainGame(WIDTH, HEIGHT, new
      SplashState()))
        game.Run();
}
```

Code Organization

There are different schools of thought when organizing code. There are a lot of projects that follow established patterns like Model/View/View-Model (MVVM) or Model/View/Controller (MVC) and group all the controllers in a directory called "controllers," models in a directory called "models," and so on. This increases the ease of finding code in the project. If a programmer is looking for a specific View, they will simply have to navigate to the View directory and look there.

Another school of thought is to organize the code by feature, with every code file related to a feature, like audio or input, to be located within the same directory. This is the school of thought we will use here as we reorganize the code. All audio, input, game state, and game object code will be colocated together. At the same time, game-specific code will be organized by which game state it belongs to. Our command mappers, game events, and game commands will all be colocated by game state.

In Figure 7-3, we see that the engine code has been moved to an Engine directory, while game-specific code has been organized by game state. We are now ready to add audio to our game in the SoundManager.cs file, located in the Sound directory of the engine.

Figure 7-3. *The resulting code tree after our reorganization*

Audio

MonoGame provides us with a simple and cross-platform API that supports mp3, ogg, and wav file formats out of the box in the content pipeline tool. We added a few more assets in the assets directory of Chapter 7. Here are the wav files for the background soundtrack that game will play:

- FutureAmbient _1.wav

- FutureAmbient _2.wav

- FutureAmbient _3.wav

- FutureAmbient _4.wav

We also added a bullet sound effect we will use when the player is shooting and an empty wav file to use when the engine cannot load a sound file:

- bullet.wav

- empty.wav

Open up the Content Pipeline Tool and add all six .wav files to the list of assets, as seen in Figure 7-4. We decided to rename the bullet and empty sounds in the pipeline to bulletSound and emptySound to make it easier to differentiate from the images of the same name.

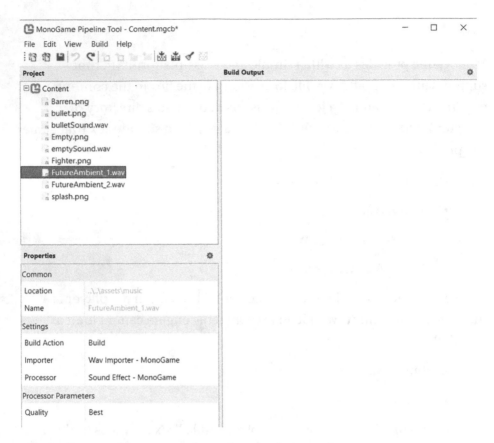

Figure 7-4. *Adding sounds to the pipeline tool*

Make sure the sounds for our new wav files use the Wav Importer and are set up as Sound Effects. In the properties box at the bottom of the pipeline tool, set the Importer to "Wav Importer – MonoGame" using the drop-down selection, and set the Processor to "Sound Effect – MonoGame" in the same way. The pipeline tool also offers importers for mp3 and ogg files, but be careful around using mp3 files since it is a proprietary format and if your game is popular you might be asked to pay royalties. The pipeline tool also offers a Sound processor, but we will discuss shortly why we chose not to use it for our background music.

Playing a Soundtrack

Unless we are creating a game scene without any background music for the effect that it has on the player, we will want to have some kind of soundtrack. We could compose our own soundtrack, we could hire a composer to create some tracks for us, we could buy songs that already exists, or we could find royalty-free music that we can legally use and redistribute. Should you decide to use music or sounds with a Creative Commons (CC) license, please double check what rights you have since there are a few variations available to creators. This last option is appealing in our case since we are building a simple game for demonstration purposes. However, one downside to doing that is that we risk having the same music as another game and that would be embarrassing. We recommend a visit to the Free Music Archive on the Internet, located here: www.freemusicarchive.org/.

We have already selected some .wav files that we want to use in our game, however, and placed them in this chapter's assets\music directory.

There are two ways to play background music using MonoGame: the MediaPlayer or using sound effects. The media player was added as a way for Xbox players to add their own background music to a game as they played, and it works great for that purpose. It evens streams the song from the disk as it plays it instead of loading the entire file in memory. To use the media player, we would need to add our tracks to the content pipeline tool and select a Sound processor. The class itself is very straightforward to use. Adding this function in the Base game state classes would let the game load a song:

```
using Microsoft.Xna.Framework.Media;
protected Song LoadContent(string songName)
{
    return _contentManager.Load<Song>(songName);
}
```

And we could then play the song like this in our game state classes:

```
var song = LoadSong("SomeSoundtrack");
MediaPlayer.Play(song);
```

The media player allows game developers to queue songs, play the next or previous song, pause and resume songs, and adjust the volume. It behaves just like... a media player!

Unfortunately, however, the media player suffers from one major downside: it adds a slight, almost half-second silence between songs, which eliminates the possibility to loop over short song samples to create a seemingly endless track. To alleviate this, we could craft a very long song that would eventually loop. The slight silence would still be noticeable, but it would not happen very often, which makes it less of a problem. Still, it would make our game feel less polished.

Our game will be using short sound samples that we will loop over. We have four such samples in our assets directory and they can be mixed together in any order. When added to the content pipeline tool, they must use a SoundEffect processor, like in Figure 7-4.

Let's add a method in our BaseGameState class to allow us to load those samples:

```
protected SoundEffect LoadSound(string soundName)
{
    return _contentManager.Load<SoundEffect>(soundName);
}
```

The return sound effect can then be used like this in the game states:

```
var sound = LoadSound("someSoundEffect");
sound.CreateInstance();
sound.Play();
```

The sound will then be audible during the game. But it will not repeat, which is what we want for sound effects, like shooting bullets, but not for

our backing tracks. Notice as well that we are calling CreateInstance()
on the loaded sound effect objects, which returns a SoundEffectInstance
object that gives use more control over the sound. A SoundEffect object
can be played and that is pretty much it, but a SoundEffectInstance object
can be played, paused, resumed, and looped. We could also change the
volume, panning, and pitch of a sound effect as it plays.

To loop over our sound sample, we just need to set the IsLooped
property to true:

```
sound.IsLooped = true;
sound.Play();
    and will play forever until it is stopped with
sound.Stop();
```

However, we do not want to keep playing the same audio sample
repeatedly, which would make our game a bit monotonic. We would like
instead to rotate over our samples and play the next one whenever the
current one stops playing. Thankfully, the SoundEffectInstance class offers
us the ability to monitor the state of a sample by reading the State property
of its objects, which can have three different values: Paused, Playing, or
Stopped.

Our strategy to rotate over song samples can now take shape. When
we initialize a game state, we will load our soundtrack samples and add
reference them in a List<SoundEffectInstance>. When the Update()
method is called by the MainGame class, we will start playing the first
sample if no music is currently playing. Otherwise, if the current track is
stopped, we will move to the next track and start playing it. This process
will repeat throughout the duration of our current game state.

We also need to keep in mind that we are creating a game engine, so
the responsibility to keep track of our samples and play them should be in
the engine itself. This is very basic functionality for a game and we would
very much like to reuse that code in our future projects.

Let's create a SoundManager class in the Engine\Sound directory:

```
public class SoundManager
{
    private int _soundtrackIndex = -1;
    private List<SoundEffectInstance> _soundtracks =
        new List<SoundEffectInstance>();
    public void SetSoundtrack(List<SoundEffectInstance> tracks)
    {
        _soundtracks = tracks;
        _soundtrackIndex = _soundtracks.Count - 1;
    }

    public void PlaySoundtrack()
    {
        var nbTracks = _soundtracks.Count;

        if (nbTracks <= 0)
        {
            return;
        }

        var currentTrack = _soundtracks[_soundtrackIndex];
        var nextTrack = _soundtracks[(_soundtrackIndex + 1) %
            nbTracks];

        if (currentTrack.State == SoundState.Stopped)
        {
            nextTrack.Play();
            _soundtrackIndex++;

            if (_soundtrackIndex >= _soundtracks.Count)
            {
                _soundtrackIndex = 0;
            }
```

```
        }
    }
}
```

When we instantiate the sound manager, we need to give it a list of tracks that it will rotate over. It then sets the _soundtrackIndex to the last item in the list because when we tell it to play our tracks it will first move forward in the list and that would cause it to loop back over to the first SoundEffectInstance of our list.

Calling PlaySoundTrack() is where the magic happens. First, if there are not tracks in our playlist, then there is nothing to do and the method exists. Otherwise, we look at the current track and find our next track in the list. If the current track is stopped, we play the next track and increment our index. Finally, if the index has moved off the list, we reset it to the first element.

Now we can modify our GamePlayState class to use the sound manager. First in the BaseGameClass, add the following protected variable so all our game state classes have access to the sound manager:

```
protected SoundManager _soundManager = new SoundManager();
```

Then, in the LoadContent() method, add the following lines at the end:

```
var track1 = LoadSound("FutureAmbient_1").CreateInstance();
var track2 = LoadSound("FutureAmbient_2").CreateInstance();
_soundManager.SetSoundtrack(new List<SoundEffectInstance>() {
track1, track2 });
```

Since all our game states will try to loop on the music playlist, we should ideally handle the call to the sound manager to loop to the next song in the BaseGameState class every time the Update() function is called. But there is a catch… The Update() function in the base class is virtual, which means that it is only the Update() function in the child classes like GameplayState that gets called. We could add a base.

Update(gameTime) line in all our child state classes, but that defeats the purpose of having an engine and it is bad design as well. Our child classes would need to be aware that they need to call the base class's method of the same name if they want the music to keep playing. Child classes should not know that sort of implementation details, so we need a different strategy. Instead, we create a new abstract method on BaseGameState that will be called by Update():

```
public abstract void UpdateGameState(GameTime gameTime);
public void Update(GameTime gameTime)
{
    UpdateGameState(gameTime);
    _soundManager.PlaySoundtrack();
}
```

Update is still called constantly by MainGame.cs. It now also interacts with the sound manager to keep that background music playing, and it asks each child class like GameplayState and SplashState to implement their own UpdateGameState functions so they have a chance to update the game state as time goes on.

Another neat feature of this design is that each game state class can have their own soundtracks and their own rotation over the loops. If we decide to add a boss battle, it would be a new game state and you can bet that its soundtrack would be... epic!

Sound Effects

Now that we have some music playing in the background, it is time to add sound effects when our fighter shoots bullets.

Sound effects have the same copyright restrictions that soundtracks have, so we also need to be careful to either find sound recordings that are we are free to use or record our own. In this case, we decided to download a bullet sound from http://freesound.org, a website that specializes in...

well, free sounds. The bullet wav file that we added to the pipeline tool higher up uses the Creative Commons 0 license, which allows us to do whatever we want with the sound. We have also edited the sound a little to shorten it. You can do this sort of thing using Audacity (`www.audacityteam.org/`), a free open source audio editor.

Back in our project, since we already have a sound manager, we are going to update it to handle sound effects by firing game events that it can respond to. When a game state is loaded up, it will have to load all the sounds that will be needed into a sound bank and associate each sound with an event type. The game state will then listen for game events and forward them to the sound manager, who will be able to respond by playing the appropriate sound sample. We are going to need some game events to respond to, so let's start here.

We already have an enum called Events that we could use. The game already uses it and fires a GAME_QUIT event when the player presses the ESC key, but there is one problem with it. If we add another element to this enum called PLAYER_SHOOTS, then the enum becomes game specific and cannot be used in an engine because our next game might not involve a player shooting anything. It could be a chess game for all we know. So, if this enum cannot be used in an engine, then our sound manager, which is part of the engine, is not allowed to use it. Once again, we have some refactoring to do!

In the engine, add a BaseGameStateEvent class in the Engine\States directory:

```
public class BaseGameStateEvent
{
    public class GameQuit : BaseGameStateEvent { }
}
```

This will be the base class for all our game state events and we are going to follow the same pattern we used for our Input Commands, where all the public classes explicitly belong to a game state as part of their type.

Here the only common event we can think of that will be part of every future game we create is the event that will let someone quit the game.

We can now get rid of the old Events enum and update these lines of HandleInput() function in GameplayState

```
if (cmd is GameplayInputCommand.GameExit)
{
    NotifyEvent(Events.GAME_QUIT);
}
```

with this

```
if (cmd is GameplayInputCommand.GameExit)
{
    NotifyEvent(new BaseGameStateEvent.GameQuit());
}
```

and change the NotifyEvent() method and all the methods that it calls to take our new BaseGameStateEvent as a parameter instead of the Events enum.

Now we are ready to update our sound manager. Open up the SoundManager class and add the following code to it. First, we'll need a dictionary to map event types to sound effects:

```
private Dictionary<Type, SoundEffect> _soundBank = new
Dictionary<Type, SoundEffect>();
```

We also need a method to allow a game state to load up sounds into the sound bank:

```
public void RegisterSound(BaseGameStateEvent gameEvent,
SoundEffect sound)
{
    _soundBank.Add(gameEvent.GetType(), sound);
}
```

Finally, we are going to a method to allow a game state to trigger a sound to be played, based on a game event:

```
public void OnNotify(BaseGameStateEvent gameEvent)
{
    if (_soundBank.ContainsKey(gameEvent.GetType()))
    {
        var sound = _soundBank[gameEvent.GetType()];
        sound.Play();
    }
}
```

Now let's create a couple of events for our GameplayState. Create a new class in the States\Gameplay directory called GamePlayEvents:

```
public class GameplayEvents : BaseGameStateEvent
{
    public class PlayerShoots : GameplayEvents { }
}
```

And update the GameplayState class to fire up this event when the player presses the spacebar to shoot bullets. In the Shoot() private method, inside the block of code that creates the bullet game objects, call NotifyEvent():

```
if (!_isShooting)
{
    CreateBullets();
    _isShooting = true;
    _lastShotAt = gameTime.TotalGameTime;

    NotifyEvent(new GameplayEvents.PlayerShoots());
}
```

Update NotifyEvent to call the sound manager:

```
protected void NotifyEvent(BaseGameStateEvent gameEvent)
{
    OnEventNotification?.Invoke(this, gameEvent);

    foreach (var gameObject in _gameObjects)
    {
        gameObject.OnNotify(gameEvent);
    }

    _soundManager.OnNotify(gameEvent);
}
```

Finally, update the gameplay state's LoadContent() method to load the bullet sound effect and add it to the sound bank:

```
public override void LoadContent()
{
    // Code omitted for brevity
    var bulletSound = LoadSound("bulletSound");
    _soundManager.RegisterSound(new GameplayEvents.
    PlayerShoots(), bulletSound);
}
```

Notice that we are not calling CreateInstance() on this sound effect after loading it because we do not really need to pause or stop the sound effects at this time.

Summary

And there we have it. There is a looping soundtrack in our game that is unique to each game state and each soundtrack can be composed of many sound samples ordered at the desire of the game developer. We also added a sound manager to our game engine and hooked up sound effects to game events. Finally, we reorganized quite a bit of code and refactored logic that didn't make as much sense as it did when we began, which is a fact of life for software developers.

The final version of the code for this chapter can be found here: https://github.com/Apress/monogame-mastery/tree/master/chapter-07/end.

In the next chapter, we will add particle effects to the game. Our fighter jet will be able to shoot missiles that leave a trail behind them.

CHAPTER 8

Particles

You would be hard pressed to find a game without particles these days. Even simple 2D games like ours now use particles to embellish the visual effects seen on the screen – anything from a torch flickering in a hallway to a water fountain in the middle of a stunning garden. A developer could even create a flock of birds or a school of fish using such systems, with each particle being a bird or fish.

The idea behind particle engines is to generate hundreds or even thousands of particle game objects that have certain attributes like color, opacity, or scale and have these attributes change over the lifetime of the particle. Most often, a single particle will only live for a few seconds and slowly fade out of view as its opacity diminishes to the point where it is completely transparent and invisible. Every time the game's update function is called, a few dozen particles are created at a certain location on the screen and are given a direction to fly toward at a certain velocity. Just like other particle attributes, that direction can change over time, taking the particle toward an ever-evolving path. For example, firework sparks would be pulled down by gravity, even when they are shot out from the center of the explosion toward the sky.

Look at Figure 8-1. Particles are emitted from the bright white center of the fire in a circular fashion before being slowly taken by an upward force. Each particle is a semitranslucent circle that starts white and becomes

© Jarred Capellman, Louis Salin 2020
J. Capellman and L. Salin, *MonoGame Mastery*,
https://doi.org/10.1007/978-1-4842-6309-9_8

yellow and then red as it moves away from the center. Particles also have varying sizes, and the further up they go, the more transparent they become.[1]

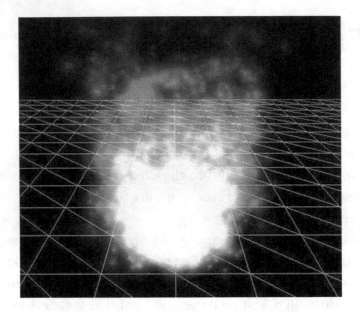

Figure 8-1.   *Fire using particles*

In this chapter, you will

- Learn about particles

- Experiment with an online particle system editor

- Build a particle system for our game

- Add missiles with a smoke trail to the game

---

[1]Image source: https://en.wikipedia.org/wiki/Particle_system#/media/
File:Particle_sys_fire.jpg

Anatomy of a Particle

What is a particle? It is a game object that will be rendered by our game engine, just like our player sprite or the scrolling background. It has a location on the screen and a texture. However, a single particle does not make a huge impact on the visual aspect of the game. Its power comes from the concentration and blending of particles on the screen. A particle will always be moving according to the principles set by its emitter. In Figure 8-2, we can see a particle being emitted with a direction and velocity, while being subjected to a gravitational force, which is not always pointing down. The dotted line represents the particle's trajectory over its lifespan and how the particle fades over time. This single particle p is represented as it ages through ages 1 to 4. It is also worth noting that the size of the particle increases as well, and it seems to be accelerating.

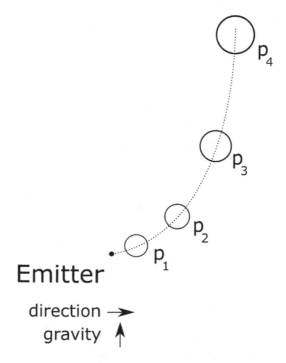

Figure 8-2. *The changes of a particle as it ages*

As the particle ages, its new position is calculated by adding the direction vector to the gravity vector and multiplying the result by the current particle velocity. This will result in a vector that, when added to the particle's current position, will give us the next location of the particle. Then, the current velocity of the particle is increased by multiplying it by an acceleration value, which we will discuss further down.

Learning with an Online Particle Editor

Sometimes the best way to learn is to experiment. There are a few online particle editors on the Internet that can help us understand what we will need to work into our game. The interesting thing about editors is that they are all slightly different in the way they generate particles. Figure 8-3 shows us an online editor with many different parameters and sliders used to manipulate particle attributes.

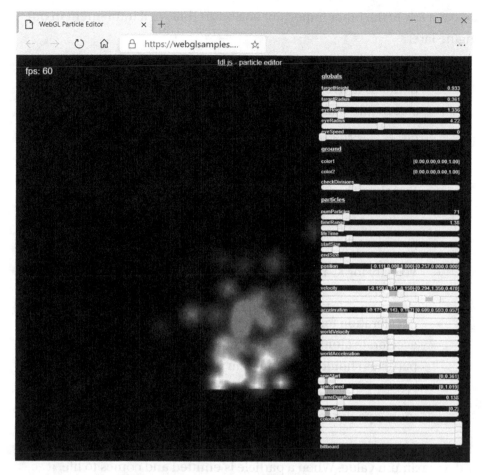

Figure 8-3. A WebGL online particle editor (`https://webglsamples.org/particleeditor/particleeditor.html`)

The first attribute we can modify under the "particles" section is the number of particles we want in our system. The more particles we have, the more concentrated they will be, and we eventually start losing the individual particles and only see a big blob of light that changes color. Let's look at a few of the other important attributes that we'll implement in our engine later:

- Lifetime: It is important to codify how long we want our particles to live so old particles can disappear for the screen and make way for new ones.

- Start size: The starting size of the particle when it is created. The size will change later as the particle ages.

- End size: The final size of the particle.

- Position range for X, Y, and Z axis: The position of the particles when they are created.

- Velocity for X, Y, and Z axis: The initial speed of the particles.

- Acceleration for X, Y, and Z axis: How the particles accelerate along all three axes. With a value of 0, particles should maintain their initial velocity.

- Opacity: As particles age, they can fade or become more opaque.

Some of the attributes in this editor are ranges with a minimum and a maximum value. When a particle is emitted and comes to life, it will be given a random value within the defined range. That little bit of randomness helps create something that looks more natural.

Try to tweak all those parameters and make this particle system look like a flame.

Different Shapes of Particle Emitters

The online particle editor that we looked at did not have an option to change the shape that the particles create. Instead, it generates particle on the floor plane around its origin and lets the particles be taken by upward and side forces. If we wanted to generate fireworks or a ring of fire, we would need something else. The particle system that we will build will take into consideration different shapes when creating particles.

Adding a Particle System to Our Game

The first use of a particle system in our game will be to generate a trail of smoke at the end of missiles that the player can shoot. Figure 8-4 shows us what this will look like.

Figure 8-4. *Player shooting a missile*

In future chapters, we will use our particle system to add sparks when an enemy is hit and explosions when various aircrafts, including our own player, get destroyed. Since explosions, sparks, and trails of smoke all take various kinds of shapes, we need to build something that can handle all those scenarios.

One thing we need to be aware of when building a particle system is that the sheer amount of game objects that can be added to the game very quickly can be enough to cause performance issues. To mitigate potential issues, we will limit the number of particles that will be emitted. Then, as particles reach their maximum lifespan or as they disappear offscreen, we will not destroy them. Instead, we will deactivate them to prevent them from being rendered and add them to a list of deactivated particles. When new particles are needed by the emitter, it will be able to reuse existing, deactivated particles and reactivate them with new reinitialized parameters. This avoids the extra cost of creating objects within the game.

Let's start by taking a look at what classes we will add to our game engine to support generating thousands of game objects that each has their own rules for moving around the screen.

Particle

We cannot have a particle system without particles! This is going to be a simple class that limits itself to holding a few of the parameters we examined earlier and it also has the responsibility of updating itself every time the game calls the Update() method. Here are the attributes the particle class keeps track of:

- Lifespan: A particle has a lifespan, which will be an integer and increase by one every time the Update() function is called. Since MonoGame calls Update() 60 times per seconds, we can easily calculate how long we want particles to last for. For example, if we wanted a particle to last 3 seconds, we would set its lifespan to 180.

- Direction: A particle has an initial direction that was set by the emitter. As it ages, it will tend to move in that direction, but will also be influenced by its gravity, velocity, and acceleration.

- Velocity: This attribute is the initial speed at which the particle is "thrown" out of the emitter. This velocity will change over time. At each update, this value will change by multiplying the current velocity to the acceleration attribute.

- Gravity: Gravity is an external force that changes the direction of the particle over time. If this force was pointing downward, then it would act as the real-life gravity that we are used to. But in particle systems, gravity can point in any direction and can be used to cause particles to float up toward the sky, or to simulate a wind draft when gravity suddenly goes sideways.

- Acceleration: This represents the acceleration of the particle as it ages. Because it is multiplied to the velocity at each update to compute a new velocity, a value between 0 and 1 will cause the velocity to become smaller over time, causing the particle to slow down as it ages. A value greater than 1 will cause the particle to pick up speed throughout its life.

- Rotation: Even though we will write some code to track a rotation value, we will not use rotation at this time in our game. We are adding it here because we may need it in future chapters and the cost of implementing it is low. Normally, a particle's sprite can rotate as the particle ages and this value is used to represent the current particle rotational angle.

- Age: The age of the particle, in number of frames. We increment this number every time the Update() method is called. When working with MonoGame, this method is called 60 times per second.

- Position: The current position of our particle in the game. It determines where the particle will be drawn on the screen.

- Opacity: Is our particle transparent, opaque, or somewhere in between? This attribute is a value between 0 and 1, with 0 indicating that the particle is fully transparent, while a value of 1 means that our particle should be drawn completely opaque.

- OpacityFadingRate: Like acceleration, this attribute determines how quickly the opacity will change as the particle ages. A value between 0 and 1 will cause the opacity to slowly diminish over time, because it will be multiplied to the current opacity value. Similarly, a value above 1 will cause the opacity to increase at each update.

- Scale: Particles can grow or shrink over time and this attribute is used to track the current scale of the particle. We will use this to scale down our game texture to fit our needs. There is no plan in this chapter to change the scale as the particle ages.

Let's take a look at our particle class:

```
public class Particle
{
    public Vector2 Position { get; private set; }
    public float Scale { get; private set; }
    public float Opacity { get; private set; }

    private int _lifespan;
    private int _age;
    private Vector2 _direction;
```

```
private Vector2 _gravity;
private float _velocity;
private float _acceleration;
private float _rotation;
private float _opacityFadingRate;

public Particle() { }

public void Activate(int lifespan, Vector2 position,
    Vector2 direction,
    Vector2 gravity,
    float velocity, float acceleration,
    float scale, float rotation, float opacity,
    float opacityFadingRate)
{
    _lifespan = lifespan;
    _direction = direction;
    _velocity = velocity;
    _gravity = gravity;
    _acceleration = acceleration;
    _rotation = rotation;
    _opacityFadingRate = opacityFadingRate;
    _age = 0;

    Position = position;
    Opacity = opacity;
    Scale = scale;
}
```

```
    // Returns false if it went past its lifespan
    public bool Update(GameTime gameTime)
    {
        _velocity *= _acceleration;
        _direction += _gravity;

        var positionDelta = _direction * _velocity;

        Position += positionDelta;

        Opacity *= _opacityFadingRate;

        // Returns true if particle can stay alive
        _age++;
        return _age < _lifespan;
    }
}
```

Of all our attributes, Position, Opacity, and Scale are set as properties with public getters because the Emitter will be responsible for drawing them and it will need to access these values.

The Update() method is called 60 times per second and will, at every call, update the position, opacity, and age of the particle. First, the velocity is multiplied by the acceleration, either slowing down or speeding up the particle. Then, as seen in Figure 8-5, a new direction vector of the particle, d', is calculated by adding the gravity vector g to the current direction vector d. d' becomes the new direction for this particle. Given enough time passes, the direction will eventually match gravity and point in the same direction.

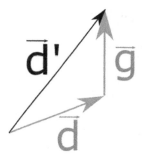

Figure 8-5. *Adding vectors d and g together creates a new vector d.'*

When multiplied by the velocity, the new direction vector grows and gives us the new particle position once added to the particle's current position. Right after this, we tweak the opacity by multiplying it with the opacityFadingRate, and finally, we increase the age of the particle.

The Update() method will return true if the particle should stay alive because it hasn't reached its maximum lifespan yet. Once it returns false, it will be a signal for the emitter to deactivate it and stop drawing it on the screen.

EmitterParticleState

The responsibility of this class is to store all the initial parameters needed by the emitter to create a new particle. While the particle class itself keeps track of most of the same attributes as the change, the EmitterParticleState class is used to store the original values needed to create each new particle. What is also interesting here is that this class allows for a certain variation in the values it stores. Lifespan, for example, has a min and max value, and some attributes like velocity and opacity have associated deviation attributes that will be used to generate values later.

The attributes this class tracks are

- MinLifeSpan
- MaxLifeSpan
- Velocity
- VelocityDeviation
- Acceleration
- Gravity
- Opacity
- OpacityDeviation
- OpacityFadingRate
- Rotation
- RotationDeviation
- Scale
- ScaleDeviation

Each of these attributes is made available to users of the class via abstract property getters that must be overridden by child classes.

It also has a few utility functions used to generate the initial values that are needed when creating a particle. Because we want our particles to be slightly different from each other, we add a randomness element whenever a value is generated. For example, a new lifespan for a new particle will be random and fall in between the min and max values defined earlier. In the same way, the initial velocity of a particle will be random, but between the velocity minus half the deviation, and the velocity plus half the deviation:

particle velocity = random(velocity – deviation / 2,

velocity + deviation / 2)

The result of doing this is the generated particles that fly out of the emitter at slightly different speeds, resulting in a particle engine that appears slightly more natural. Here is the code, with a RandomNumberGenerator class included for a few helper functions:

```
public class RandomNumberGenerator
{
    private Random _rnd;

    public RandomNumberGenerator()
    {
        _rnd = new Random();
    }

    public int NextRandom() => _rnd.Next();
    public int NextRandom(int max) => _rnd.Next(max);
    public int NextRandom(int min, int max) => _rnd.Next(min, max);

    public float NextRandom(float max) =>
        (float)_rnd.NextDouble() * max;
    public float NextRandom(float min, float max) =>
        ((float)_rnd.NextDouble() * (max - min)) + min;
}

public abstract class EmitterParticleState
{
    private RandomNumberGenerator _rnd = new
    RandomNumberGenerator();

    public abstract int MinLifespan { get; }
    public abstract int MaxLifespan { get; }

    public abstract float Velocity { get; }
    public abstract float VelocityDeviation { get; }
```

```
public abstract float Acceleration { get; }
public abstract Vector2 Gravity { get; }

public abstract float Opacity { get; }
public abstract float OpacityDeviation { get; }
public abstract float OpacityFadingRate { get; }

public abstract float Rotation { get; }
public abstract float RotationDeviation { get; }

public abstract float Scale { get; }
public abstract float ScaleDeviation { get; }

public int GenerateLifespan()
{
    return _rnd.NextRandom(MinLifespan, MaxLifespan);
}

public float GenerateVelocity()
{
    return GenerateFloat(Velocity, VelocityDeviation);
}

public float GenerateOpacity()
{
    return GenerateFloat(Opacity, OpacityDeviation);
}

public float GenerateRotation()
{
    return GenerateFloat(Rotation, RotationDeviation);
}
```

```
public float GenerateScale()
{
    return GenerateFloat(Scale, ScaleDeviation);
}

protected float GenerateFloat(float startN, float deviation)
{
    var halfDeviation = deviation / 2.0f;
    return _rnd.NextRandom(startN - halfDeviation, startN +
    halfDeviation);
}
}
```

IEmitterType

Emitters can come in multiple shapes. Do we want our particles to fly out in the shape of a ring or a cone, or maybe even a square? We need a way for our emitters to know where to position the initial particles and what direction they should start going to. Figure 8-6 illustrates a few types of emitters.

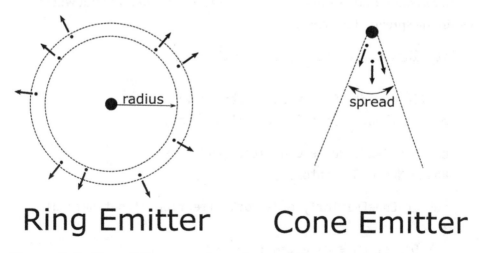

Figure 8-6. *Two different emitter shapes*

This IEmitterType interface is simple and provides two functions to get a particle position and a particle direction.

```
public interface IEmitterType
{
    Vector2 GetParticleDirection();
    Vector2 GetParticlePosition(Vector2 emitterPosition);
}
```

GetParticlePosition() will compute a new particle's position depending on the position of the emitter itself. We want new particles to be generated close to their emitters.

ConeEmitterType

Our game will create a smoke trail so our game engine will provide us with an emitter that generates particles in the shape of a cone. The cone will implement the IEmitterType interface and will have two new attributes: a direction and a spread, indicating how wide the cone is. Whenever a particle is generated, the code will position it at the same location as the emitter's center and its direction will be randomly generated but will fit within the spread of the cone.

```
public class ConeEmitterType : IEmitterType
{
    public Vector2 Direction { get; private set; }
    public float Spread { get; private set; }

    private RandomNumberGenerator _rnd = new
    RandomNumberGenerator();

    public ConeEmitterType(Vector2 direction, float spread)
    {
        Direction = direction;
```

```
        Spread = spread;
    }

    public Vector2 GetParticleDirection()
    {
        if (Direction == null)
        {
            return new Vector2(0, 0);
        }

        var angle = (float) Math.Atan2(Direction.Y, Direction.X);
        var newAngle = _rnd.NextRandom(angle - Spread / 2.0f,
            angle + Spread / 2.0f);

        var particleDirection =
            new Vector2((float)Math.Cos(newAngle),
                (float)Math.Sin(newAngle));
        particleDirection.Normalize();
        return particleDirection;
    }

    public Vector2 GetParticlePosition(Vector2 emitterPosition)
    {
        var x = emitterPosition.X;
        var y = emitterPosition.Y;

        return new Vector2(x, y);
    }
}
```

Let's take a deeper look at the GetParticleDirection() function. First, if the direction of the emitter, provided to the constructor, is null, then the direction of the particle will be (0, 0), causing it to not move. Otherwise, we calculate the angle of the emitter's direction and create a new angle for the particle within the provided spread. Armed with the new angle, we can calculate an X and Y coordinate for a particle direction vector that we then normalize, which is an operation that changes the length of the vector to 1.0. This is useful because that direction will eventually be multiplied by a particle's velocity and we do not want the direction vector to influence how fast the particle moves.

Emitter

Finally, we have the emitter itself, the central piece of this whole operation. The emitter's responsibility is to emit particles, give them their initial sets of parameters, render them on the screen, and keep track of active and inactive particles.

The emitter in our engine is a game object, meaning it has a position and a texture, which will be used to draw the particles. Every single particle emitted by this class will share the same texture and its position will be relative to the emitter's position. An emitter's position can change over time as well, like when a player carries a torch into a dark room. As such, all the particles' initial location should move along with the emitter.

```
public class Emitter : BaseGameObject
{
    private LinkedList<Particle> _activeParticles = new
        LinkedList<Particle>();
    private LinkedList<Particle> _inactiveParticles = new
        LinkedList<Particle>();
    private EmitterParticleState _emitterParticleState;
    private IEmitterType _emitterType;
    private int _nbParticleEmittedPerUpdate = 0;
    private int _maxNbParticle = 0;
```

```
    public Emitter(Texture2D texture, Vector2 position,
                EmitterParticleState particleState,
                IEmitterType emitterType, int
                nbParticleEmittedPerUpdate, int
                maxParticles)
    {
        _emitterParticleState = particleState;
        _emitterType = emitterType;
        _texture = texture;
        _nbParticleEmittedPerUpdate = nbParticleEmittedPerUpdate;
        _maxNbParticle = maxParticles;
        Position = position;
    }
    // The rest of the class is omitted while we discuss the
    // constructor
}
```

In the preceding code, we initialize an emitter with a texture, a
position, an emitter particle state, a type, the number of particles to
generate each Update() call, and the maximum number of particles this
emitter is allowed to have active at any time. Our active and inactive
particles will be tracked within two linked lists, initially empty. Linked lists
are well suited for this. When active particles die due to age, they need to
be removed from the active list and be added to the inactive list. Removing
any element from a linked list is instantaneous, which helps our engine
perform better.

Emitting a single particle happens like this:

```
private void EmitNewParticle(Particle particle)
{
    var lifespan = _emitterParticleState.GenerateLifespan();
    var velocity = _emitterParticleState.GenerateVelocity();
    var scale = _emitterParticleState.GenerateScale();
```

```
    var rotation = _emitterParticleState.GenerateRotation();
    var opacity = _emitterParticleState.GenerateOpacity();
    var gravity = _emitterParticleState.Gravity;
    var acceleration = _emitterParticleState.Acceleration;
    var opacityFadingRate = _emitterParticleState.
    OpacityFadingRate;

    var direction = _emitterType.GetParticleDirection();
    var position = _emitterType.GetParticlePosition(_position);

    particle.Activate(lifespan, position, direction, gravity,
                      velocity, acceleration, scale,
                      rotation, opacity, opacityFadingRate);
    _activeParticles.AddLast(particle);
}
```

Given a particle object that was newly instantiated and is currently inactive or active, this function will reset its attributes, activate it, and add it to the list of active particles. Every call to the _emitterParticleState here is to generate new attribute values that are within ranges defined in the particle state object given earlier to the emitter. Then we ask the emitter type for a particle position and a direction. We take all those parameters and use them to reset a particle. Then, once activated and added to the active list, this particle will be drawn on the screen and its Update() method will be called to allow it to age and change over time.

The EmitNewParticle() method is called for each particle we want to emit. Each time the Update() method is called, we want to emit _ nbParticleEmittedPerUpdate number of particles. First, we look at the list of inactive particles to see if we have any inactive particles we can reuse. If we have enough, then we simply call EmitNewParticle() for each one of those. If we do not have enough, then we create enough new particles to fill the gap and emit those as well, all while making sure we never end up with more active particles than allowed by _maxNbParticle. The main benefit of pooling our particle objects like this is to avoid the overhead of creating new instances of potentially thousands of particle game objects 60 times per second, which can slow down the game. Here, once our objects are created, they are reused and we avoid that extra computational cost.

Here is the code that handles this logic:

```
private void EmitParticles()
{
    // Make sure we're not at max particles
    if (_activeParticles.Count >= _maxNbParticle)
    {
        return;
    }

    var maxAmountThatCanBeCreated = _maxNbParticle -
        _activeParticles.Count;
    var neededParticles = Math.Min(maxAmountThatCanBeCreated,
        _nbParticleEmittedPerUpdate);

    // Reuse inactive particles first before creating new ones
    var nbToReuse = Math.Min(_inactiveParticles.Count,
     neededParticles);
    var nbToCreate = neededParticles - nbToReuse;

    for(var i = 0; i < nbToReuse; i++)
    {
        var particleNode = _inactiveParticles.First;

        EmitNewParticle(particleNode.Value);
        _inactiveParticles.Remove(particleNode);
    }
```

```
    for(var i = 0; i < nbToCreate; i++)
    {
        EmitNewParticle(new Particle());
    }
}
```

We start by calculating how many particles we can create. Of that number, we compute how many will come from the list of inactive particles and how many need to be created. For each inactive particle we are reemitting, we pluck it out of the list and use it in the EmitNewParticle() call. For each new particle we need to create, we instantiate them and use them in the same call.

We now need to call Update() on all these particles and we are going to do that in the emitter's own Update() method:

```
public void Update(GameTime gameTime)
{
    EmitParticles();

    var particleNode = _activeParticles.First;
    while (particleNode != null)
    {
        var nextNode = particleNode.Next;
        var stillAlive = particleNode.Value.Update(gameTime);
        if (!stillAlive)
        {
            _activeParticles.Remove(particleNode);
            _inactiveParticles.AddLast(particleNode.Value);
        }

        particleNode = nextNode;
    }
}
```

We immediately start by emitting particles. Then, we iterate over all our active particles and call Update() on each one of them. As mentioned when discussing the Particle class, Update() returns false if the particle has aged past its maximum age. When this happens, we remove it from the list of active particles and add it to the inactive particles list.

Finally, we can now render each active particle:

```
public override void Render(SpriteBatch spriteBatch)
{
    var sourceRectangle = new Rectangle(0, 0, _texture.Width,
        _texture.Height);

    foreach (var particle in _activeParticles)
    {
        spriteBatch.Draw(_texture, particle.Position,
                        sourceRectangle,
                        Color.White * particle.Opacity, 0.0f,
                        new Vector2(0, 0),
                        particle.Scale, SpriteEffects.None,
                        zIndex);
    }
}
```

Render() will iterate over each active particle and call one of the overloaded Draw() functions on the spriteBatch that allows us to change the scale and opacity of the particle.

This concludes the part of our particle system that we added to our game engine. We are now ready to create our smoke trail particle emitter and add it to the game!

Adding a Missile and Smoke Trail to Our Game

You can find all the code for this chapter at https://github.com/Apress/ monogame-mastery/tree/master/chapter-08/end and all the game assets here: https://github.com/Apress/monogame-mastery/tree/master/ chapter-08/assets. We added two new textures: one for our smoke trail and one for a missile. We also added a new sound effect for the missile.

The first step in adding a new kind of particle system to the game, especially one that is meant to move quickly offscreen as the missile shoots up rapidly, is to have a way to experiment with the smoke trail and observe it without it going offscreen too rapidly. Thankfully, we already have a mechanism to do this and build our new MissileSprite game object without having to care about bullets and fighter jets and our scrolling background.

The game is built by taking players from one game state to another. First, the player is shown the Splash game state, and when they press the Enter key, they get moved to the Gameplay state. What if we had a Dev game state where we can put objects on the screen and not have them move at all? This game state would be a sandbox we can play in while we build our game objects.

Creating a Dev Game State to Play With

Let's create a new folder called Dev within the States directory and add a DevInputCommand, a DevInputMapper, and a DevState.

This game state would require some input, as we want to be able to exit the state and we want to make sure the missile works well when we fire it. Here are the commands we care about:

```
public class DevInputCommand : BaseInputCommand
{
    public class DevQuit : DevInputCommand { }
    public class DevShoot : DevInputCommand { }
}
```

As in the real game, pressing the ESC key will exit the game, and pressing the spacebar will cause a missile to shoot up when we want to test that functionality:

```
public class DevInputMapper : BaseInputMapper
{
    public override IEnumerable<BaseInputCommand>
    GetKeyboardState(KeyboardState state)
    {
        var commands = new List<DevInputCommand>();

        if (state.IsKeyDown(Keys.Escape))
        {
            commands.Add(new DevInputCommand.DevQuit());
        }

        if (state.IsKeyDown(Keys.Space))
        {
            commands.Add(new DevInputCommand.DevShoot());
        }

        return commands;
    }
}
```

Let's now add our new textures to the content pipeline. We'll need two new textures, located in the chapter's asset folder in chapter-08\assets\png named Cloud001 and Missile05. Add these textures to the content pipeline and call them, respectively, Cloud and Missile. Our DevState will use the Cloud texture immediately and will eventually use the Missile texture as well.

We can now create our smoke trail particle emitter, which we simply called an exhaust. Take the following code and put it in a file called Exhaust.cs, located in a new folder called Particles:

```
public class ExhaustParticleState : EmitterParticleState
{
    public override int MinLifespan => 60; // equivalent to 1
                                           // second
    public override int MaxLifespan => 90;
    public override float Velocity => 4.0f;
    public override float VelocityDeviation => 1.0f;
    public override float Acceleration => 0.8f;
    public override Vector2 Gravity => new Vector2(0, 0);
    public override float Opacity => 0.4f;
    public override float OpacityDeviation => 0.1f;
    public override float OpacityFadingRate => 0.86f;
    public override float Rotation => 0.0f;
    public override float RotationDeviation => 0.0f;
    public override float Scale => 0.1f;
    public override float ScaleDeviation => 0.05f;
}

public class ExhaustEmitter : Emitter
{
    private const int NbParticles = 10;
    private const int MaxParticles = 1000;
    private static Vector2 Direction = new Vector2(0.0f, 1.0f);
    private const float Spread = 1.5f;
```

```
public ExhaustEmitter(Texture2D texture, Vector2 position) :
    base(texture, position, new ExhaustParticleState(),
        new ConeEmitterType(Direction, Spread),
        NbParticles, MaxParticles)
{ }
}
```

This file contains two classes: an ExhaustParticleState to track all our smoke particles' initial state and an ExhaustEmitter class, which is an emitter but also specifies how many particles to emit at every update, the maximum number of particles that we want active, the emitter's downward direction, and that we want to use the ConeEmitterType we added earlier.

Finally, let's add our DevState class, which will be used as a sandbox so that we can work on our game objects without having to deal with the entire game at the same time. The DevState, added do the States\Dev folder, looks like this:

```
public class DevState : BaseGameState
{
    private const string ExhaustTexture = "Cloud";
    private ExhaustEmitter _exhaustEmitter;

    public override void LoadContent()
    {
        var exhaustPosition = new Vector2(_viewportWidth / 2,
            _viewportHeight / 2);
        _exhaustEmitter = new ExhaustEmitter(LoadTexture
        (ExhaustTexture), exhaustPosition);
        AddGameObject(_exhaustEmitter);
    }
```

```
    public override void HandleInput(GameTime gameTime)
    {
        InputManager.GetCommands(cmd =>
        {
            if (cmd is DevInputCommand.DevQuit)
            {
                NotifyEvent(new BaseGameStateEvent.GameQuit());
            }
        });
    }

    public override void UpdateGameState(GameTime gameTime)
    {
        _exhaustEmitter.Update(gameTime);
    }

    protected override void SetInputManager()
    {
        InputManager = new InputManager(new DevInputMapper());
    }
}
```

This should start looking familiar. LoadContent() creates an exhaust emitter and puts it in the middle of the viewport and sets its texture to the Cloud texture. HandleInput() takes care of the DevQuit command by exiting the game. UpdateGameState() calls the emitter's Update() method and SetInputManager() connects our DevInputMapper class to the state's input manager.

Now we need to get the game to start with our DevState instead of the SplashState. Modify the Program.cs Main method to use the DevState as its initial state:

```
static void Main()
{
    using (var game = new MainGame(WIDTH, HEIGHT, new
            DevState()))
        game.Run();
}
```

Run the program and you should see something like Figure 8-7, with a lot of smoke particles being generated very rapidly in the shape of a cone.

Figure 8-7. *Smoke!*

So smoke is being generated, but we don't know yet what that looks like as it moves. Update the Update() method of the DevState class to do move the emitter up over time and destroy it when it goes too far offscreen:

```
public override void UpdateGameState(GameTime gameTime)
{
    _exhaustEmitter.Position =
        new Vector2(_exhaustEmitter.Position.X,
                    _exhaustEmitter.Position.Y - 3f);
    _exhaustEmitter.Update(gameTime);

    if (_exhaustEmitter.Position.Y < -200)
    {
        RemoveGameObject(_exhaustEmitter);
    }
}
```

Run the game again and we should see the smoke trail moving up. Feel free to tweak the ExhaustParticleState attributes or the ExhaustEmitter's number of particles to see how that affects the smoke trail. Finding a suitable set of parameters is tedious work where we change attributes and must run our game every time to visualize the results. No wonder there are particle engine editors out there to help! Once you are happy with what your exhaust looks like on the screen, it's time to add a missile!

This Missile will be a composite game object. It has a missile texture (the Missile texture we added to the content pipeline earlier) and the exhaustEmitter as well. That's two game objects in one, which makes sense since the two are tightly tied together. Create a new MissileSprite.cs to the Objects folder and use the following code:

```
public class MissileSprite : BaseGameObject
{
    private const float StartSpeed = 0.5f;
    private const float Acceleration = 0.15f;
```

```
private float _speed = StartSpeed;

// Keep track of scaled-down texture size
private int _missileHeight;
private int _missileWidth;

// Missiles are attached to their own particle emitter
private ExhaustEmitter _exhaustEmitter;

public override Vector2 Position
{
    set
    {
        _position = value;
        _exhaustEmitter.Position =
            new Vector2(_position.X + 18, _position.Y +
            _missileHeight - 10);
    }
}

public MissileSprite(Texture2D missleTexture, Texture2D
exhaustTexture)
{
    _texture = missleTexture;
    _exhaustEmitter = new ExhaustEmitter(exhaustTexture,
        _position);

    var ratio = (float) _texture.Height /
        (float) _texture.Width;
    _missileWidth = 50;
    _missileHeight = (int) (_missileWidth * ratio);
}
```

```
public void Update(GameTime gameTime)
{
    _exhaustEmitter.Update(gameTime);

    Position = new Vector2(Position.X, Position.Y - _speed);
    _speed = _speed + Acceleration;
}

public override void Render(SpriteBatch spriteBatch)
{
    // Need to scale down the sprite. The original texture
    // is very big
    var destRectangle =
        new Rectangle((int) Position.X, (int) Position.Y,
        _missileWidth, _missileHeight);
    spriteBatch.Draw(_texture, destRectangle, Color.White);

    _exhaustEmitter.Render(spriteBatch);
}
}
```

The main difference between this game object and others like the player sprite is that we added an exhaust emitter game object within the MissileSprite. When creating a missile, we must supply two textures: the missile texture and the smoke texture for the emitter. What's more, whenever the missile's position changes, we must update the emitter's position as well, which we take care of within the Position property setter function. Every call to the MissileSprite's Update() method also calls the emitter's Update() method, and similarly, every call to Render() will call the emitter's Render() function in addition to drawing the missile texture on the screen.

The original missile texture is very big and must be scaled down before drawing it. A width of 50 pixels seems reasonable to use here so we need to calculate the desired height of the missile, so it maintains the same width/height ration as the original texture size, which is done in the class constructor. When drawing the missile, we use a SpriteBatch draw function where we get to specify the source rectangle of the texture and the destination rectangle on the screen. If the two rectangles are not the same size, MonoGame will take care of scaling the source rectangle to the size of the destination rectangle, like illustrated in Figure 8-8.

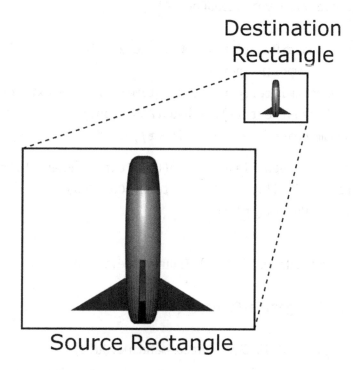

Figure 8-8. *Scaling down our missile texture*

Let's add an instance of the MissileSprite object to our DevState and see how it goes! For fun, let's also add the player sprite and play a bit with the objects in our sandbox. Change the DevState class to look like this:

```
public class DevState : BaseGameState
{
    private const string ExhaustTexture = "Cloud";
    private const string MissileTexture = "Missile";
```

```
private const string PlayerFighter = "fighter";

private ExhaustEmitter _exhaustEmitter;
private MissileSprite _missile;
private PlayerSprite _player;

public override void LoadContent()
{
    var exhaustPosition = new Vector2(_viewportWidth / 2,
        _viewportHeight / 2);
    _exhaustEmitter = new ExhaustEmitter(LoadTexture(
        ExhaustTexture), exhaustPosition);
    AddGameObject(_exhaustEmitter);

    _player = new PlayerSprite(LoadTexture(PlayerFighter));
    _player.Position = new Vector2(500, 500);
    AddGameObject(_player);
}

public override void HandleInput(GameTime gameTime)
{
    InputManager.GetCommands(cmd =>
    {
        if (cmd is DevInputCommand.DevQuit)
        {
            NotifyEvent(new BaseGameStateEvent.GameQuit());
        }

        if (cmd is DevInputCommand.DevShoot)
        {
            _missile =
                new MissileSprite(LoadTexture(MissileTexture),
                                  LoadTexture(Exhaust
                                  Texture));
```

```
            _missile.Position = new Vector2(_player.
            Position.X, _player.Position.Y - 25);
            AddGameObject(_missile);
        }
    });
}

public override void UpdateGameState(GameTime gameTime)
{
    _exhaustEmitter.Position =
        new Vector2(_exhaustEmitter.Position.X,
                    _exhaustEmitter.Position.Y - 3f);
    _exhaustEmitter.Update(gameTime);

    if (_missile != null)
    {
        _missile.Update(gameTime);

        if (_missile.Position.Y < -100)
        {
            RemoveGameObject(_missile);
        }
    }

    if (_exhaustEmitter.Position.Y < -200)
    {
        RemoveGameObject(_exhaustEmitter);
    }
}

protected override void SetInputManager()
{
    InputManager = new InputManager(new DevInputMapper());
}
}
```

We are monitoring the DevShoot command and adding a missile to the game whenever it is triggered. Immediately, the missile shoots up with some smoke trailing behind, so we can easily see the result of our work and if we are happy with it. This is not perfect game code, however. The Update() method is called 60 times per second, and even though we press the spacebar only once, it remains pressed for a few of those frames and multiple missiles are thus created, but all of them are stored in the same _missile private variable, causing some visual artifacts. Also, the missile isn't centered on the player sprite, as we can see in Figure 8-9. But let's not waste any effort solving this here, in the sandbox. We will devote our time fixing these issues in the real game.

Figure 8-9. *Adding game objects to our sandbox, with interesting visual artifacts*

Adding the Missile Game Object to Our Game

To get started adding the missiles to our game, we first need to revert Program.cs to load up the GameplayState class upon startup.

```
static void Main()
{
    using (var game = new MainGame(WIDTH, HEIGHT, new
            SplashState()))
        game.Run();
}
```

We want our missiles to fire only once per second, as the player presses the spacebar, while bullets are being shot at the same time. This is to prevent the player from firing too many missiles. We also need to add a sound effect for the missile. Open the content pipeline and follow the same steps we used in the previous chapter for the bullet sound effects. Add the assets\sounds\missile wav file and call it missileSound. Make sure to use the Wav Importer and the Sound Effect processor. Save and build the content pipeline before returning to the code.

In the GameplayState class, add these private variables:

```
private const string ExhaustTexture = "Cloud";
private const string MissileTexture = "Missile";
private Texture2D _missileTexture;
private bool _isShootingMissile;
private TimeSpan _lastMissileShotAt;
private List<MissileSprite> _missileList;
```

We will follow the same pattern we used for shooting bullets. When we fire a missile, the _isShootingMissile Boolean variable will be set to true to prevent us from firing any more missiles. Every second, that variable will be set to false so we can fire them again. We will also keep track of missiles on the screen using _missileList, so we can update and render them.

Now update LoadContent() to load the missile texture and the missile sound effect, which needs to be added to the sound bank of our sound manager.

185

```
_missileTexture = LoadTexture(MissileTexture);
_exhaustTexture = LoadTexture(ExhaustTexture);
_missileList = new List<MissileSprite>();

var missileSound = LoadSound("missileSound");
_soundManager.RegisterSound(
    new GameplayEvents.PlayerShootsMissile(), missileSound,
    0.4f, -0.2f, 0.0f
);
```

We need to add a new GameplayEvent so the sound manager knows to play the missile sound effect whenever we shoot a missile. Update the GameplayEvents class so it looks like this:

```
public class GameplayEvents : BaseGameStateEvent
{
    public class PlayerShootsBullets : GameplayEvents { }
    public class PlayerShootsMissile : GameplayEvents { }
}
```

The Shoot() method is called whenever the player presses the spacebar. Add the following code to it. It should look very similar to the code we used to shoot bullets:

```
if (!_isShootingMissile)
{
    CreateMissile();
    _isShootingMissile = true;
    _lastMissileShotAt = gameTime.TotalGameTime;

    NotifyEvent(new GameplayEvents.PlayerShootsMissile());
}
```

The CreateMissile() function is new and should look like this, creating, positioning, and adding missiles to the list of game objects:

```
private void CreateMissile()
{
    var missileSprite = new MissileSprite(_missileTexture,
        _exhaustTexture);
    missileSprite.Position =
        new Vector2(_playerSprite.Position.X + 33,
        _playerSprite.Position.Y - 25);

    _missileList.Add(missileSprite);
    AddGameObject(missileSprite);
}
```

Just like bullets, as missiles go offscreen, they need to be removed from the list of game objects. We already have code to clean up bullets in the UpdateGameState() function, and cleaning missiles will look very similar. Instead of duplicating that code for missiles, we now have the opportunity to create a new method that will clean bullets and missiles. Take the cleaning code from UpdateGameState(), parametrize it so any BaseGameObject can be cleaned up, and move that logic to a new method called CleanObjects:

```
private List<T> CleanObjects<T>(List<T> objectList) where T :
BaseGameObject
{
    List<T> listOfItemsToKeep = new List<T>();
    foreach(T item in objectList)
    {
        var stillOnScreen = item.Position.Y > -50;
```

```
    if (stillOnScreen)
    {
        listOfItemsToKeep.Add(item);
    }
    else
    {
        RemoveGameObject(item);
    }
}

return listOfItemsToKeep;
}
```

We can now update UpdateGameState() to move missiles on the screen by calling their Update() method, make sure we cannot fire them more than once per second, and clean them up after they are off the screen:

```
public override void UpdateGameState(GameTime gameTime)
{
    foreach (var bullet in _bulletList)
    {
        bullet.MoveUp();
    }

    foreach (var missile in _missileList)
    {
        missile.Update(gameTime);
    }
    // Can't shoot bullets more than every 0.2 second
    if (_lastBulletShotAt != null &&
        gameTime.TotalGameTime - _lastBulletShotAt > TimeSpan.
        FromSeconds(0.2))
```

```
    {
        _isShootingBullets = false;
    }

    // Can't shoot missiles more than every 1 second
    if (_lastMissileShotAt != null &&
        gameTime.TotalGameTime - _lastMissileShotAt > TimeSpan.
        FromSeconds(1.0))
    {
        _isShootingMissile = false;
    }

    // Get rid of bullets and missiles that have gone out of view
    _bulletList = CleanObjects(_bulletList);
    _missileList = CleanObjects(_missileList);
}
```

With those modifications done, you can launch the game and see that the player can shoot bullets and missiles at the same time!

Summary

You can spend a lot of time tweaking particle engines and emitter parameters to achieve desired effects. In this chapter, we developed our own particle engine to generate a trail of smoke behind missiles being fired by our player. The effect adds a little sophistication to the game, but it could be better. For example, using linear transformations to update parameters like opacity or velocity over time could be made better by using tween curves, where an attribute's value over time follows a curve instead of a straight line. Other improvements would be to implement particle rotation and scale over time, having particles change color, using multiple textures for different particles, or even having particle textures morph over time via an animation as they age.

Adding the particle engine was a lot of work, but seeing that smoke trail behind our missiles is very neat and adds a bit of realism to our game. We also got to experience our engine and how it made it simple to create a sandbox that we, the developers, can use to experiment and build new game objects that once created can easily be added to the gameplay state.

In the next chapter, we will work on collision detections. What could collide together in our game? Our bullets and... enemies!

CHAPTER 9

Collision Detection

Think of a video game without collision detection in some shape or form. It's difficult! Collision detection is ubiquitous and part of many aspects that make up a game. Is the player standing on a platform or should they be falling? How can we prevent the player from stepping beyond the edge of the world map? Did the player get hit by a swirling hammer? Were we successful in picking up the shiny coins? All those things are decided by collision detection. This is what we will explore in this chapter. How can we detect if two objects collided with each other, and what should be done when those collisions happen? One other interesting use case for collision detection is to detect what game object a player clicked using the mouse or their finger.

If you think about it, we already implemented a naïve form of collision detection in the game when we checked each update if the player runs out of bounds. We are essentially detecting a collision with the edges of the screen and preventing the player sprite from progressing further.

We have spent some time refactoring our code for this chapter and we will not detail all of those changes here. Some modifications were made as we identified areas of the program with duplicated logic, or the need to change our particle Emitter class to allow it to stop emitting particles without removing the emitter from the game objects, so as to allow existing particles to fade off instead of being abruptly removed from the screen. As always, you can download the code we started with here: `https://github.com/Apress/monogame-mastery/tree/master/chapter-09/start`. The final code, including the collision detection

© Jarred Capellman, Louis Salin 2020
J. Capellman and L. Salin, *MonoGame Mastery*,
https://doi.org/10.1007/978-1-4842-6309-9_9

logic, is here: https://github.com/Apress/monogame-mastery/tree/
master/chapter-09/end. All changes we made will be present in the end
project.

Figure 9-1 gives us a glimpse of what our game will look like at the end
of this chapter.

Figure 9-1. *The final results*

Now let's get started! In this chapter, you will

- Review a few collision detection algorithms used today
  in video games

- Add enemy choppers to the game, giving the player
  something to shoot at

- Add a collision detector to the engine and destroy some
  enemies

Techniques

Collision detection is such a vast topic that entire books have been written about it. We will explore the basic concepts about it and a few algorithms before settling with how we are going use it in our game.

Whether two things collide is entirely based on the concept of bounding boxes which are a simpler way to represent game objects for the purpose of calculating if they collide with each other. Visually, humans can easily see if two objects came into contact. However, computers have a harder time at this so we must help them. Bounding boxes are named this way because they most often represent the outermost bounds of the object and are usually rectangles in two dimensions, or boxes in three dimensions. Look at Figure 9-2. On the left, we see our player sprite and an enemy helicopter. Do they collide? How would you write an algorithm to detect that they do? On the right side of the image, you see the same object, with their bounding boxes drawn. This way of representing objects makes it much easier and faster to detect that two objects intersect. It may not be perfect, but it works well enough for most purposes where perfect accuracy isn't a requirement.

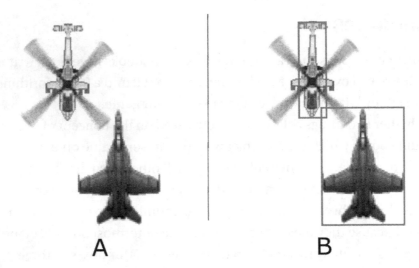

Figure 9-2. *Is our fighter sprite colliding with the chopper? Yes, it is!*

We have a slight problem here. Although we can now detect collisions between objects by looking if their bounding boxes intersect, we might detect collisions that are not really happening, like in the previous image. There are a few ways to mitigate that. First, rectangles do not have a monopoly here. We could as well have a bounding sphere or circle if our game object fits that shape better. Second, as we will implement later in this chapter, we can also have multiple bounding boxes, as seen in Figure 9-3. Using more than one box to define the contour of our game objects makes it easier to fit the shape that we want to match, but it does add a bit of extra work because it is one extra box we need to check for each game object on the screen.

Figure 9-3. *Is our fighter sprite colliding with the chopper? Not this time.*

Any object that can collide with another object must have a bounding box of some sort, or some bounds of a different shape like a sphere or cone. If we have hundreds or thousands of objects in the game, like spark particles that fall to the floor and are not allowed to go through the floor, which algorithm should we use to handle all those collisions? Let's review a few.

AABB (Axis Aligned Bounding Box)

So far, the bounding boxes we have looked at have all been aligned on the X and Y axis, with their sides completely horizontal and vertical. Computing two aligned axis bounding boxes is straightforward: given box A and box B, their (x, y) position, and their (width, height) dimensions, the two boxes intersect if

- A.x <= B.x + B.width and

- A.x + A.width >= B.x and

- A.y <= B.y + B.height and

- A.y + A.height >= b.height

See Figure 9-4 for a visual representation of these four conditions.

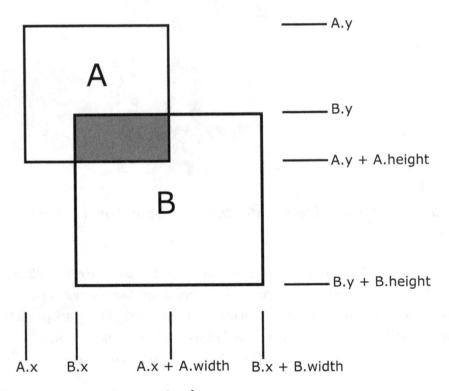

Figure 9-4. *Two intersecting boxes*

OBB (Oriented Bounding Box)

Oriented bounding boxes are like the aligned axis boxes earlier, but they can be rotated as the game object rotates, making the calculation to detect collisions a bit more complicated. Given two bounding boxes A and B, for

196

each axis, which are X and Y in a two-dimensional game, project all the corners of the bounding box A to that axis and only keep the smallest and largest points. Now do the same for bounding box B. Look at Figure 9-5 for an example of projecting the bounding box corners to the X axis.

Now the calculation is similar to AABB.

If the following is true for *all* axes, then we have a collision if

- A-min <= B-max

- B-min <= A-max

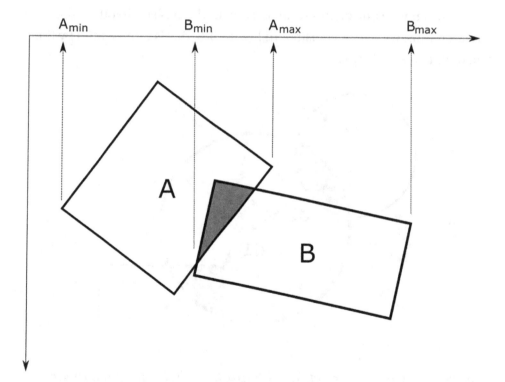

Figure 9-5. *Oriented bounding boxes intersecting*

Spheres

Should you choose to use spheres, or circles in a 2D game, then you might need to calculate if your sphere intersects with other spheres or rectangles. In Figure 9-6, the middle circle is intersecting with the other circle and the rectangle. Two circles or spheres collide when the distance between their center is smaller than the sum of their radii. In Figure 9-6, the two circles collide because d2 is smaller than r1 + r2.

When looking if a rectangle collides with a circle, calculate the distance between the center of the circle and the closest point of the rectangle, which may not be one of the corners. If any of them is smaller than the circle's radius, we have a collision. In Figure 9-6, this is represented by the fact that d1 is smaller than r1.

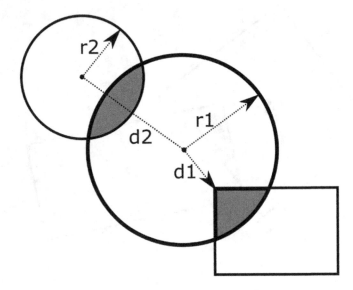

Figure 9-6. *Circle intersecting with another circle and a rectangle*

Uniform Grids

So far, our strategy has been to collect all the objects on the screen and see which objects collide with which objects. This might be fine if we only have a few objects to look at, but as the number of objects grows, the number of calculations also grows exponentially. For example, with 100 objects on the screen, we will perform at most 100^2 collision detections. Since we run this at every Update() method call, this means we need to be able to do this 60 times per second, or our game risks slowing down.

To help reduce the number of checks that we do each frame, a few algorithms have been designed to arrange our objects in a spatial data structure, so we know which objects are near each other. Then, we only need to check for collisions between neighboring objects, saving us a lot for compute time. The only downside to these next few algorithms is that arranging objects in the data structures takes time, but hopefully not as much as it would to run a brute-force collision detection algorithm.

With that said, let's start with uniform grids, which are a 2D array in which each cell is initially empty and has a width and a height. The grid cells, if we ever bothered to draw them on the screen, should fill up the viewport. Then, we take all our game objects and figure out which cells they overlap. For each one of those cells, we add a link to the game object. When all the game objects have been processed, we go through each cell and see which ones link to more than one object. When that happens, we perform collision detection on the linked objects to see the bounding boxes or spheres intersect. See Figure 9-7 for an example.

How wide and tall each cell depends entirely on the game developer. Since the goal is to minimize the number of calculations we ultimately must perform, having more cells will reduce the possibility that they have more than one object linked in them. However, it may cause the same objects to be linked in many cells. On the other hand, if the cells are too big, we are back at square one if all the game objects end up in the same cell and we have to brute force our way through collision detection. As you can see in Figure 9-7, collision detection for the two circles will happen six times because that many cells link to the two objects. Since we only need to perform collision detection once, the programmer will need to make sure to only perform this action once per game object pairs.

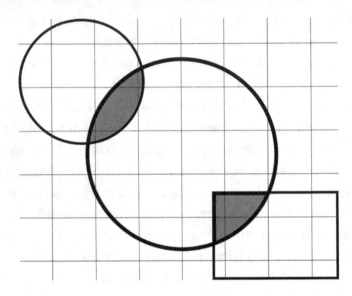

Figure 9-7. *Imagining our objects if they were drawn on a uniform grid*

Quadtrees

Quadtrees are a variation on uniform grids, but instead of using a 2D array as a data structure to link game objects together, we use a tree where each node has either zero or four children. When instantiating a new quadtree, we pass in as a parameter the size of our viewport and the maximum number of game objects that a node can store. The tree will initially create its root node, which covers the entire screen, and we then can add our game objects to the tree, one by one. Objects are added to the root node until we reach the maximum number of objects per node, at which point the quadtree will subdivide itself and create four children empty nodes and move all game objects in the root nodes to the children nodes, based on where they belong. If a game object overlaps two nodes, it is then stored in the parent node. The process then repeats until all objects have been processed. As each node is created, it knows precisely what parts of the screen it covers by keeping track of its top-left corner coordinates, its width, and its height.

Figure 9-8 provides an example of a quadtree that has a maximum node capacity of one, meaning that the nodes will subdivide into four whenever there are two or more objects in them. First, the square is put into the root node. Then the circle is added, which means the root node has two objects and must subdivide itself into four other children nodes. The square is moved to the node that represents the top-left quadrant. The circle, however, overlaps two quadrants, so it will remain in the root node. Finally, the small rectangle is added to the first quadrant, which causes it to split into four. The bigger rectangle remains in its node because it overlaps the children nodes, while the smaller rectangle is put into the fourth child quadrant.

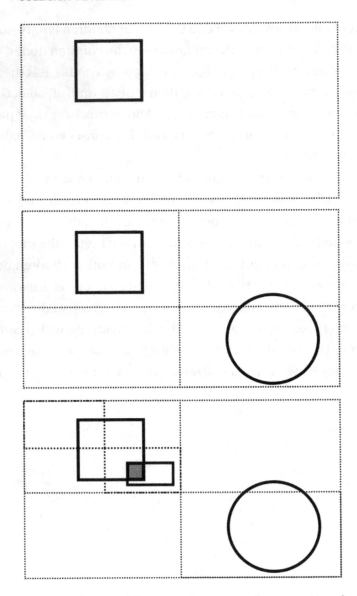

Figure 9-8. *A quadtree with a maximum node capacity of one*

To perform collision detection, we loop over our game objects and ask the quadtree for all objects that belong in the same node or in children nodes. We then perform collision detection between those objects only.

Other Techniques

There are many other techniques out there used both to perform collision detection and to optimize the performance of all these calculations. We discussed a few of them in this section, but we encourage you to explore this world of possibilities to find what suits your needs. From the different kinds of tree structures to 3D algorithms and rendering-based approaches, there are many tools at our disposal.

Adding Enemies to Our Game

Before we implement collision detection in our game, we need things to collide with. And because we are implementing a vertical shooter game, most collisions are going to be between bullets and enemies. So, we need enemies!

We added two new images to the assets\png directory:

- One image with a few different colored helicopters: chopper-44x99.png

- A new explosion texture that we will use for a new particle emitter when enemies (or the player) die: explosion.png

Add the two new images to the content pipeline tool and name the helicopter image in the tool to chopper.png. Save and build the content pipeline.

We can now create our new chopper enemy game object and use the first helicopter texture from that chopper image. Although there are many different choppers in the image, including two different kinds of blades, we will use only the first yellow helicopter and add the blurry blades and make them rotate over time. To do so, we will use the version of the SpriteBatch Render method that allows us to pick a specific region of the source image that we want to render to the screen. This way, we can select the yellow chopper and the blurry blades and render the two on top of each other on the screen.

Let's create the ChopperSprite class into a new file in the Objects directory:

```
public class ChopperSprite : BaseGameObject
{
    // Which chopper do we want from the texture
    private const int ChopperStartX = 0;
    private const int ChopperStartY = 0;
    private const int ChopperWidth = 44;
    private const int ChopperHeight = 98;

    // Where are the blades on the texture
    private const int BladesStartX = 133;
    private const int BladesStartY = 98;
    private const int BladesWidth = 94;
    private const int BladesHeight = 94;

    // Rotation center of the blades
    private const float BladesCenterX = 47.5f;
    private const float BladesCenterY = 47.5f;

    // Positioning of the blades on the chopper
    private const int ChopperBladePosX = ChopperWidth / 2;
    private const int ChopperBladePosY = 34;

    private int _life = 40;

    public ChopperSprite(Texture2D texture)
    {
        _texture = texture;
    }
```

```
public override void OnNotify(BaseGameStateEvent gameEvent)
{
    switch (gameEvent)
    {
        case GameplayEvents.ChopperHitBy m:
            JustHit(m.HitBy);
            SendEvent(new GameplayEvents.EnemyLostLife
            (_life));
            break;
    }
}

private void JustHit(IGameObjectWithDamage o)
{
    _hitAt = 0;
    _life -= o.Damage;
}
}
```

There is a lot going on here. We are keeping track of the position of our desired chopper from the texture, the position of the blurry blades, where we want the blades to be positioned on top of the chopper, and the center position of the blades when we rotate them. We are also keeping track of life points on the chopper. As it gets hit by bullets and missiles, its life total will drop until it reaches zero, at which point it will get removed from the game and replaced by an explosion particle emitter. Each chopper object will react to a new ChopperHitBy gameplay event that tells it a game object that implements the IGameObjectWithDamage interface just hit it. The interface, seen in the code below, offers a Damage property that the chopper will use to reduce its life total. After being hit, the chopper will send out a notification that its own state has changed, which will let the GameplayState class react to the chopper's death by removing it from the game and replacing it with an explosion particle emitter.

```
public interface IGameObjectWithDamage
{
    int Damage { get; }
}
```

We now need to be able to render our chopper on the screen, but we have a small problem… The helicopters in the texture are all facing upward, but if our enemies are going to come down into the viewport and attacking our player, they should be facing down. We need to rotate them around.

Rotating Our Chopper

Rotation is not a complicated thing to do, as MonoGame supports this out of the box. But we need to know where the rotation center is. If we don't specify it, MonoGame will assume that the rotation center is the same as the origin of the texture, which means the (0, 0) coordinates. Figure 9-9 shows an example of what the rendering would look like if we rotated the chopper 180 degrees without changing the rotation center. We can see the original chopper, facing up, and the rotated chopper. This isn't a big deal in and of itself, but we'll need to add spinning blades on this rotated enemy and rotating the helicopter around the (0, 0) origin makes it hard to figure out where to position the blades texture. Instead, what we want to do is rotate the chopper around a better rotation center, which could be exactly where the blades need to go.

Figure 9-9. *Rotating our helicopter 180 degrees around its (0, 0) origin*

We can start working on our Render method:

```
public override void Render(SpriteBatch spriteBatch)
{
    var chopperRect =
        new Rectangle(ChopperStartX, ChopperStartY,
        ChopperWidth, ChopperHeight);
    var chopperDestRect =
        new Rectangle(_position.ToPoint(), new
        Point(ChopperWidth, ChopperHeight));

    var color = Color.White;
    spriteBatch.Draw(_texture, chopperDestRect, chopperRect,
                     color, MathHelper.Pi,
                     new Vector2(ChopperBladePosX,
                     ChopperBladePosY), SpriteEffects.None, 0f);
}
```

The preceding code calculates the source rectangle of our yellow helicopter body on the original image and the destination rectangle on the screen where we want the chopper to be drawn. We then draw the enemy and rotate it 180 degrees by using the angle in radians as the fifth parameter to spriteBatch.Draw. 180 degrees in radian is PI, so we use MonoGame's MathHelper.Pi property here.

Spinning Blades

Let's add some spinning blades. First, we need to specify the speed at which the blades spin, in radians. We will use that number to increment the rotation angle of the blades every time the Render() method is called.

```
private const float BladeSpeed = 0.2f;
private float _angle = 0.0f;
```

Now we need to add the spinning blade to the chopper. Add the following code to the Render() method:

```
var bladesRect = new Rectangle(BladesStartX, BladesStartY,
    BladesWidth, BladesHeight);
var bladesDestRect = new Rectangle(_position.ToPoint(), new
    Point(BladesWidth, BladesHeight));

spriteBatch.Draw(_texture, bladesDestRect, bladesRect, Color.
                White, _angle,
                new Vector2(BladesCenterX, BladesCenterY),
                SpriteEffects.None, 0f);

_angle += BladeSpeed;
```

The preceding code is similar to what we did to render the rotated chopper, except that we provide the _angle variable to the Draw() method and increment the angle by the BladeSpeed constant at every frame.

Making the Choppers Move

To make our chopper move across the screen, we will provide them with a path via a constructor parameter, which is a list of frame numbers and direction vectors. The sprites will make their way into the screen from the left or the right side of the viewport, and after a certain number of frames, they will change their direction and move down diagonally. To implement this, let's add a speed variable to our object and add that path to the constructor. Then, when the Update() method is called, we will calculate the age of the game object in number of frames elapsed since it was created and compare that age with the path the chopper must take, and change the chopper direction accordingly. First, we need some class variables:

```
private const float Speed = 4.0f;
private Vector2 _direction = new Vector2(0, 0);
private int _age = 0;

private List<(int, Vector2)> _path;
```

The _path variable stores tuples of the type (int, Vector2), which represent the frame number and associated direction.

Change the constructor to take in a path:

```
public ChopperSprite(Texture2D texture, List<(int, Vector2)> path)
{
    _texture = texture;
    _path = path;
}
```

And add an Update method that can be called by our GameplayState class:

```
public void Update()
{
    // Choppers follow a path where the direction changes at a
    // certain frame,
    // which is tracked by the chopper's age
    foreach(var p in _path)
    {
        int pAge = p.Item1;
        Vector2 pDirection = p.Item2;

        if (_age > pAge)
        {
            _direction = pDirection;
        }
    }

    Position = Position + (_direction * Speed);

    _age++;
}
```

Feel free to experiment with this new game object in the DevState class, our sandbox state class that we created in the previous chapter, to get a feel for how the chopper can move across the screen! Give them a path and make sure to call Update on them.

To generate the choppers from the left and right side of the screen, we create a ChopperGenerator class responsible for creating the ChopperSprite game objects and setting them offscreen on the left or right. In the following code, the generator is instantiated with the helicopter texture, the number of choppers to generate, and a handler that the game state class will use to receive a notification that a chopper was created, so it can have a chance to update its list of enemies and add the objects to the active game object list. When GenerateChoppers() is called, the generator will create a chopper every 500 milliseconds, alternating between positioning it on the left or on the right of the screen. It will also create a path for the chopper and assign it.

```
public class ChopperGenerator
{
    private bool _generateLeft = true;
    private Vector2 _leftVector = new Vector2(-1, 0);
    private Vector2 _downLeftVector = new Vector2(-1, 1);
    private Vector2 _rightVector = new Vector2(1, 0);
    private Vector2 _downRightVector = new Vector2(1, 1);

    private Texture2D _texture;
    private System.Timers.Timer _timer;
    private Action<ChopperSprite> _chopperHandler;
    private int _maxChoppers = 0;
    private int _choppersGenerated = 0;
    private bool _generating = false;

    public ChopperGenerator(Texture2D texture, int nbChoppers,
    Action<ChopperSprite> handler)
    {
        _texture = texture;
        _chopperHandler = handler;

        _downLeftVector.Normalize();
        _downRightVector.Normalize();

        _maxChoppers = nbChoppers;
```

```
    _timer = new System.Timers.Timer(500);
    _timer.Elapsed += _timer_Elapsed;
}

public void GenerateChoppers()
{
    if (_generating)
    {
        return;
    }

    _choppersGenerated = 0;
    _timer.Start();
}

public void StopGenerating()
{
    _timer.Stop();
    _generating = false;
}

private void _timer_Elapsed(object sender,
    System.Timers.ElapsedEventArgs e)
{
    List<(int, Vector2)> path;
    if (_generateLeft)
    {
        path = new List<(int, Vector2)>
        {
            (0, _rightVector),
            (2 * 60, _downRightVector),
        };
```

```
        var chopper = new ChopperSprite(_texture, path);
        chopper.Position = new Vector2(-200, 100);
        _chopperHandler(chopper);
    }
    else
    {
        path = new List<(int, Vector2)>
        {
            (0, _leftVector),
            (2 * 60, _downLeftVector),
        };

        var chopper = new ChopperSprite(_texture, path);
        chopper.Position = new Vector2(1500, 100);
        _chopperHandler(chopper);
    }

    _generateLeft = !_generateLeft;

    _choppersGenerated++;
    if (_choppersGenerated == _maxChoppers)
    {
        StopGenerating();
    }
    }
}
```

In our GameplayState class, let's add the choppers to an enemy list and get them to start moving. We can also add a new explosion particle emitter while we are there, which we will look at in the next section. For now, however, we can look at how we are handling it here. There were some changes made to the particle emitter class that we will not go over in here to allow the game state class to stop an emitter without destroying it:

```
public class GameplayState : BaseGameState
{
    // ...
    private const string ChopperTexture = "Chopper";
    private const string ExplosionTexture = "explosion";
    private const int MaxExplosionAge = 600; // 10 seconds at
                                             // 60 frames per
                                             // second = 600
    // Emit particles for 1.2 seconds and let them fade out for
    // 10 seconds
    private const int ExplosionActiveLength = 75;
    private Texture2D _chopperTexture;

    private List<ExplosionEmitter> _explosionList = new
        List<ExplosionEmitter>();
    private List<ChopperSprite> _enemyList = new
        List<ChopperSprite>();

    public override void LoadContent()
    {
        _explosionTexture = LoadTexture(ExplosionTexture);
        _chopperTexture = LoadTexture(ChopperTexture);
        _chopperGenerator = new ChopperGenerator(_
        chopperTexture, 4, AddChopper);
        _chopperGenerator.GenerateChoppers();
    }

    public override void UpdateGameState(GameTime gameTime)
    {
        // ...
        foreach (var chopper in _enemyList)
```

```
    {
        chopper.Update();
    }
    _enemyList = CleanObjects(_enemyList);
}

private void AddChopper(ChopperSprite chopper)
{
    chopper.OnObjectChanged +=
        _chopperSprite_OnObjectChanged;
    _enemyList.Add(chopper);
    AddGameObject(chopper);
}

private void AddExplosion(Vector2 position)
{
    var explosion = new ExplosionEmitter(_explosionTexture,
        position);
    AddGameObject(explosion);
    _explosionList.Add(explosion);
}

private void UpdateExplosions(GameTime gameTime)
{
    foreach (var explosion in _explosionList)
    {
        explosion.Update(gameTime);

        if (explosion.Age > ExplosionActiveLength)
        {
            explosion.Deactivate();
        }
```

```
        if (explosion.Age > MaxExplosionAge)
        {
            RemoveGameObject(explosion);
        }
    }
  }
}
```

Note that in the AddChopper() method, we are registering to an event that has been added to the BaseGameObject. Individual game objects, like the ChopperSprite, can trigger this event when their internal state changes. We will be using this event further below, when we handle enemies losing all their life total.

We are also keeping track of all the explosions added to the game and updating them so the particles can be emitted. Once an explosion reaches a certain age, it stops emitting particles, which causes the existing ones to fade away for a while, until the emitter reaches its maximum age and is removed from the game.

Adding an Explosion Particle Engine

Now that we can add enemies to our game, enemies that we can shoot and destroy, we'll need a new particle emitter so we can have at least some rudimentary explosion when enemies (or the player) die.

Explosions are not cone shaped. Instead, particles should be generated within a circle and grow over time. To achieve this, we need a new emitter type that does not have a direction and will generate particles within a given radius. Add this class to the Engine\Particles\EmitterTypes directory:

```
public class CircleEmitterType : IEmitterType
{
    public float Radius { get; private set; }
```

```csharp
private RandomNumberGenerator _rnd = new
RandomNumberGenerator();

public CircleEmitterType(float radius)
{
    Radius = radius;
}

public Vector2 GetParticleDirection()
{
    return new Vector2(0f, 0f);
}

public Vector2 GetParticlePosition(Vector2 emitterPosition)
{
    var newAngle = _rnd.NextRandom(0, 2 * MathHelper.Pi);
    var positionVector = new Vector2(
        (float)Math.Cos(newAngle),
        (float)Math.Sin(newAngle));
    positionVector.Normalize();

    var distance = _rnd.NextRandom(0, Radius);
    var position = positionVector * distance;

    var x = emitterPosition.X + position.X;
    var y = emitterPosition.Y + position.Y;

    return new Vector2(x, y);
}
}
```

Then, in our games Particles\ directory, add an Explosion.cs file and add the following code to it:

```
public class ExplosionParticleState : EmitterParticleState
{
    public override int MinLifespan => 180; // equivalent to 3
                                            // seconds

    public override int MaxLifespan => 240;

    public override float Velocity => 2.0f;

    public override float VelocityDeviation => 0.0f;

    public override float Acceleration => 0.999f;

    public override Vector2 Gravity => new Vector2(0, 1);

    public override float Opacity => 0.4f;

    public override float OpacityDeviation => 0.1f;

    public override float OpacityFadingRate => 0.92f;

    public override float Rotation => 0.0f;

    public override float RotationDeviation => 0.0f;

    public override float Scale => 0.5f;

    public override float ScaleDeviation => 0.1f;
}

public class ExplosionEmitter : Emitter
{
    private const int NbParticles = 2;
    private const int MaxParticles = 200;
```

```
private const float Radius = 50f;

public ExplosionEmitter(Texture2D texture, Vector2
position) :
    base(texture, position, new ExplosionParticleState(),
    new CircleEmitterType(Radius),
        NbParticles, MaxParticles) { }
}
```

We added a gravity direction to our particles so the cloud of explosion textures drifts slightly toward the bottom to create the illusion of movement. You can add an instance of the ExplosionEmitter into the DevState and see how it performs on its own. In the game, when an enemy dies, we will remove the chopper game object from the list of active game objects and replace it with an explosion emitter. That will generate particles for a few seconds before stopping.

Adding Collision Detection

We are now ready to add logic to our game to detect the following collisions:

- Are any bullets hitting an enemy?

- Are any missiles hitting an enemy?

- Is any enemy colliding with the player sprite?

Given that our game does not have a huge number of objects at any given time, maybe dozens of bullets, a few enemies, and eventually their own projectiles, we can afford to use the brute-force method of performing collision detection on every pair of objects in the game. We can be smart about it, however, because we know that bullets will never intersect with each other. We also do not really care if missiles hit bullets. We already maintain a list of bullets and a list of missiles in our GameplayState class. It would be trivial to reuse those lists and add a new enemy list and perform collision detection between two lists of game objects: one list of passive objects, like bullets, and a list of active objects that will be notified when they get hit.

Bounding Boxes

To perform collision detection between game objects, we need bounding boxes, and MonoGame provides out-of-the-box support for bounding boxes via the BoundingBox class in the Microsoft.Xna.Framework namespace. That class gives us a few utility functions like merging two bounding boxes into one, creating bounding boxes out of spheres, and computing if two bounding boxes intersect with each other, which would result in a collision. Unfortunately for our 2D game, the MonoGame BoundingBox class uses three-dimensional vectors, which means its main use is for 3D games. Although it would be possible to use the class in a 2D game, the idea of remembering to set everything on the z=0 plane to get rid of the third dimension is not very appealing. This is why we will build our own 2D BoundingBox class for our game.

Add the following class in Engine\Objects:

```
public class BoundingBox
{
    public Vector2 Position { get; set; }
    public float Width { get; set; }
    public float Height { get; set; }

    public Rectangle Rectangle
    {
        get
```

```
        {
            return new Rectangle((int)Position.X, (int)
            Position.Y, (int)Width, (int)Height);
        }
    }

    public BoundingBox(Vector2 position, float width,
    float height)
    {
        Position = position;
        Width = width;
        Height = height;
    }

    public bool CollidesWith(BoundingBox otherBB)
    {
        if (Position.X < otherBB.Position.X + otherBB.Width &&
            Position.X + Width > otherBB.Position.X &&
            Position.Y < otherBB.Position.Y + otherBB.Height &&
            Position.Y + Height > otherBB.Position.Y)
        {
            return true;
        }
        else
        {
            return false;
        }
    }
}
```

Our BoundingBox class is built using a position on the screen, a width, and a height. We also provide a utility Rectangle property that converts our box into a rectangle, which we will use later to visualize our boxes on the screen. This is useful when we need to debug why our bounding boxes do not appear to be at the right place. Finally, the class offers a utility function that returns true when it intersects with another bounding box.

We now need to update our game objects to add bounding boxes. If you remember Figure 9-3 earlier in the chapter, we were describing using one box for the chopper and two boxes for the player sprite. We'll also need to add a bounding box to our bullets and missiles. Since a few game objects require the use of bounding boxes, it makes sense to add that functionality in the base class. Open up BaseGameObject and add the following code:

```
protected List<BoundingBox> _boundingBoxes = new
List<BoundingBox>();

public List<BoundingBox> BoundingBoxes
{
    get
    {
        return _boundingBoxes;
    }
}

public virtual Vector2 Position
{
    get { return _position; }
    set
    {
        var deltaX = value.X - _position.X;
        var deltaY = value.Y - _position.Y;
        _position = value;
```

```
        foreach(var bb in _boundingBoxes)
        {
            bb.Position = new Vector2(bb.Position.X + deltaX,
            bb.Position.Y + deltaY);
        }
    }
}

public void AddBoundingBox(BoundingBox bb)
{
    _boundingBoxes.Add(bb);
}

public void RenderBoundingBoxes(SpriteBatch spriteBatch)
{
    if (_boundingBoxTexture == null)
    {
        CreateBoundingBoxTexture(spriteBatch.GraphicsDevice);
    }

    foreach (var bb in _boundingBoxes)
    {
        spriteBatch.Draw(_boundingBoxTexture, bb.Rectangle,
        Color.Red);
    }
}
```

Our game objects can now add bounding boxes to a list, tracked by the base class. That list will be available to our game state classes to perform collision detection. We also updated the Position property so that when it changes, we also change the position of the bounding box on the screen. Finally, we can also render the boxes on the screen, very simply as big red rectangles, making it easy for developers to see immediately if their boxes are at the right position and follow the objects as they move.

Let's see what adding bounding boxes looks like for our chopper game object:

```
private int BBPosX = -16;
private int BBPosY = -63;
private int BBWidth = 34;
private int BBHeight = 98;

public ChopperSprite(Texture2D texture, List<(int, Vector2)>
path)
{
    _texture = texture;
    _path = path;
    AddBoundingBox(new Engine.Objects.BoundingBox(
        new Vector2(BBPosX, BBPosY), BBWidth, BBHeight));
}
```

That's it! Adding a bounding box to an object is as easy as calling AddBoundingBox for each box we want to add. The BaseGameObject will take care of the rest.

You may notice that the BBPosX and BBPosY variables are negative, which means the bounding box is off the screen. That is because initially, the chopper's position is at (0, 0) and we then rotate it 180 degrees around its origin, causing the sprite to be rotated offscreen. Instead of writing rotation code to similarly rotate the bounding box to the same position, we took the liberty of modifying the box's position directly in the variables.

Our player, bullet, and missile game objects have similar logic, but you may wonder how we came up with the bounding boxes values. We can easily figure out the position, width, and height of a bounding box by opening the texture in a graphical tool like Photoshop or even Paint that gives us pixel coordinates as we hover the mouse over the loaded image. Except for the missile texture, which is scaled down at rendering time, our bounding boxes can be fetched using those tools directly.

```
public class BulletSprite : BaseGameObject ,
IGameObjectWithDamage
{
    private const int BBPosX = 9;
    private const int BBPosY = 4;
    private const int BBWidth = 10;
    private const int BBHeight = 22;

    public int Damage => 10;

    public BulletSprite(Texture2D texture)
    {
        _texture = texture;
        AddBoundingBox(
            new Engine.Objects.BoundingBox(new Vector2
            (BBPosX, BBPosY), BBWidth, BBHeight));
    }
}
```

Notice that the bullet class now implements the IGameObjectWithDamage interface, so it must have a Damage property, which returns 10. The missile class further below will also have this interface, but its damage is slightly higher at 25.

```
public class PlayerSprite : BaseGameObject
{
    private const int BB1PosX = 29;
    private const int BB1PosY = 2;
    private const int BB1Width = 57;
    private const int BB1Height = 147;

    private const int BB2PosX = 2;
    private const int BB2PosY = 77;
    private const int BB2Width = 111;
```

```csharp
    private const int BB2Height = 37;

    public PlayerSprite(Texture2D texture)
    {
        _texture = texture;
        AddBoundingBox(
            new Engine.Objects.BoundingBox(new Vector2(BB1PosX,
            BB1PosY), BB1Width, BB1Height));
        AddBoundingBox(
            new Engine.Objects.BoundingBox(new Vector2(BB2PosX,
            BB2PosY), BB2Width, BB2Height));
    }
}

public class MissileSprite : BaseGameObject ,
IGameObjectWithDamage
{
    private int _missileHeight;
    private int _missileWidth;

    public int Damage => 25;

    public MissileSprite(Texture2D missleTexture, Texture2D
    exhaustTexture)
    {
        _texture = missleTexture;
        _exhaustEmitter = new ExhaustEmitter(exhaustTexture,
            _position);

        var ratio = (float) _texture.Height /
                    (float) _texture.Width;
        _missileWidth = 50;
        _missileHeight = (int) (_missileWidth * ratio);
```

```
    // Note that the missile is scaled down! So its
    // bounding box must be scaled down as well
    var bbRatio = (float) _missileWidth / _texture.Width;

    var bbOriginalPositionX = 352;
    var bbOriginalPositionY = 7;
    var bbOriginalWidth = 150;
    var bbOriginalHeight = 500;

    var bbPositionX = bbOriginalPositionX * bbRatio;
    var bbPositionY = bbOriginalPositionY * bbRatio;
    var bbWidth = bbOriginalWidth * bbRatio;
    var bbHeight = bbOriginalHeight * bbRatio;

    AddBoundingBox(
        new Engine.Objects.BoundingBox(new
        Vector2(bbPositionX, bbPositionY), bbWidth,
        bbHeight));
    }
}
```

It is worth spending a few moments on the missile bounding boxes. The original missile texture is much larger than how we want them drawn and is scaled down at rendering time. To compute its rendering box, we fetch the position, width, and height from the original image and multiplied those values by the scaling ratio to get new values that fit the scaled-down missile texture.

To visualize the bounding boxes, we can add a _debug variable to BaseGameState that defaults to false:

```
protected bool _debug = false;
```

and use it in the rendering code:

```
public void Render(SpriteBatch spriteBatch)
{
    foreach (var gameObject in _gameObjects.OrderBy(a =>
    a.zIndex))
    {
        gameObject.Render(spriteBatch);

        if (_debug)
        {
            gameObject.RenderBoundingBoxes(spriteBatch);
        }
    }
}
```

This will cause the game engine to draw the bounding boxes on top[1] of the game objects each frame if the _debug flag is turned on, as seen in Figure 9-10, where we can see that all bounding boxes are positioned and scaled properly.

---

[1]We updated the code in Chapter 10 to draw the bounding boxes underneath the game objects instead as this makes things easier to visualize.

Figure 9-10. *Drawing the bounding boxes on top of game objects for debug purposes*

AABB Collision Detection

We are now ready to detect collisions. Since we are going to do AABB-style collision detection, add a class in Engine\Objects called AABBCollisionDetector:

```
public class AABBCollisionDetector<P, A>
    where P : BaseGameObject
    where A : BaseGameObject
{
    private List<P> _passiveObjects;

    public AABBCollisionDetector(List<P> passiveObjects)
    {
        _passiveObjects = passiveObjects;
    }
```

```
public void DetectCollisions(A activeObject, Action<P, A>
collisionHandler)
{
    foreach(var passiveObject in _passiveObjects)
    {
        if (DetectCollision(passiveObject, activeObject))
        {
            collisionHandler(passiveObject, activeObject);
        }
    }
}

public void DetectCollisions(List<A> activeObjects,
Action<P, A> collisionHandler)
{
    foreach(var passiveObject in _passiveObjects)
    {
        foreach(var activeObject in activeObjects)
        {
            if (DetectCollision(passiveObject,
            activeObject))
            {
                collisionHandler(passiveObject,
                activeObject);
            }
        }
    }
}

private bool DetectCollision(P passiveObject, A
activeObject)
{
    foreach(var passiveBB in passiveObject.BoundingBoxes)
```

```
    {
        foreach(var activeBB in activeObject.BoundingBoxes)
        {
            if (passiveBB.CollidesWith(activeBB))
            {
                return true;
            }
        }
    }

    return false;
    }
}
```

This class is instantiated with a list of passive objects, like bullets, that we will use later to check for collisions with a single active object or a list of active objects, by using the two overloaded DetectCollisions() methods. Both methods will iterate over each passive object and active object and check for collisions using the AABB algorithm we discussed higher in the chapter. When a collision is detected, a collisionHandler handler function is called and both colliding objects are passed in as parameters, giving an opportunity to the caller to react to each collision.

In the GameplayState class, add the following code to the UpdateGameState() method:

```
DetectCollisions();
```

And implement that DetectCollisions() method:

```
private void DetectCollisions()
{
    var bulletCollisionDetector =
        new AABBCollisionDetector<BulletSprite,
        ChopperSprite>(_bulletList);
```

```
    var missileCollisionDetector =
        new AABBCollisionDetector<MissileSprite,
        ChopperSprite>(_missileList);
    var playerCollisionDetector =
        new AABBCollisionDetector<ChopperSprite,
        PlayerSprite>(_enemyList);

    bulletCollisionDetector.DetectCollisions(
        _enemyList, (bullet, chopper) =>
    {
        var hitEvent = new GameplayEvents.ChopperHitBy(bullet);
        chopper.OnNotify(hitEvent);
        _soundManager.OnNotify(hitEvent);
        bullet.Destroy();
    });

    missileCollisionDetector.DetectCollisions(_enemyList,
        (missile, chopper) =>
    {
        var hitEvent = new GameplayEvents.ChopperHitBy(missile);
        chopper.OnNotify(hitEvent);
        _soundManager.OnNotify(hitEvent);
        missile.Destroy();
    });

    playerCollisionDetector.DetectCollisions(_playerSprite,
        (chopper, player) =>
    {
        KillPlayer();
    });
}
```

First, we build three distinct collision detectors, one for each of the scenarios we are interested in. Then, we call DetectCollisions() for each of our scenarios:

- Bullets hitting choppers

- Missile hitting choppers

- Choppers hitting the player

We also pass in a lambda function as our handler to react to collisions. When bullets or missiles hit choppers, we generate a new gameplay event and notify the chopper, who will then update its own life total. We also notify the sound manager in case we have a sound effect that needs to be played. Finally, instead of removing the colliding bullet or missile from the game, we mark it as destroyed. The CleanObject method was updated to also clean up destroyed objects, so marked objects are removed at every Update() call.

We also need to respond to the choppers' life total changing. When it reaches zero, we want to remove the chopper and replace it by an explosion. We do this in the following method that we linked with the chopper's OnObjectChanged event:

```
private void _chopperSprite_OnObjectChanged(object sender,
BaseGameStateEvent e)
{
    var chopper = (ChopperSprite)sender;
    switch (e)
    {
        case GameplayEvents.EnemyLostLife ge:
            if (ge.CurrentLife <= 0)
            {
                AddExplosion(new Vector2(chopper.Position.X -
                    40, chopper.Position.Y - 40));
                chopper.Destroy();
```

```
        }
        break;
    }
}
```

Here, we destroy the chopper if its life total is zero or less, meaning that the CleanObjects() method will take care of removing it from the game the next time it is called. We then call AddExplosion(), which will create a nice little explosion on the screen exactly where the chopper used to be.

Finally, the KillPlayer() function is implemented like this:

```
private async void KillPlayer()
{
    _playerDead = true;

    AddExplosion(_playerSprite.Position);
    RemoveGameObject(_playerSprite);

    await Task.Delay(TimeSpan.FromSeconds(2));
    ResetGame();
}
```

The player is marked as dead to prevent it from shooting bullets. An explosion is positioned on top of the player sprite just before removing the game object from the game. Then, we give the player two seconds to realize what just happened and we reset the game so the level can start over.

Load up the chapter-9 end solution in Visual Studio and give it a try!

Summary

In this chapter, we looked at a few different algorithms for performing collision detection and how we can hook them into our gameplay code and react to collisions. Enemies can get hit by bullets and missiles, lose life, and eventually explode into a cloud of fire.

We have done a lot in this chapter, but unfortunately, we could not look in detail at all the code that was added, like how the choppers briefly change color when hit by bullets or how the game resets to reload the level. We encourage you to investigate this on your own and we believe that you currently have all the tools you need to implement this at home. When developing a video game, the devil is in the details: we could spend more time adding spark particles to choppers when they get hit. We could use an OBB-style collision detection and rotate the choppers when they move diagonally. We should probably add sound effects when bullets hit choppers or when they explode. We are also at the point where we need to add lives to the player so we can retry the level three times before we are game over.

The thing is, however, that you now have all the tools you need to implement those details. What is missing is the ability to add text to the game and display the player's remaining lives. We will get to that one in a future chapter, but before that, we'd like to move on to another interesting subject: animation!

CHAPTER 10

Animations and Text

Unless you are building a *Tetris* clone or a text-based game, like the classic game *Zork*, you will need animations in your video game to make it feel more fluid. Even the 1978 game *Space Invaders* had a very basic and crude animation, where enemies provide the illusion of movement by switching between two sprites every second or so: at one moment the aliens' arms are down and the next second the arms are up. Animations provide us with the illusion of life.

Another topic that has been missing in our game so far is text. Every single game has some form of text. Even when the gameplay has no text, which is rare, games usually have some form of menu system where the player can choose between items like "Start Game," "Continue," or "Quit." In the archetype that we are modeling our game after, players have a fixed number of lives and can accumulate a score, where both are displayed on the screen.

Figure 10-1 gives us an example of the text we will have in our game by the end of the chapter.

© Jarred Capellman, Louis Salin 2020
J. Capellman and L. Salin, *MonoGame Mastery*,
https://doi.org/10.1007/978-1-4842-6309-9_10

Figure 10-1. *Text!*

In this chapter, you will

- Learn the basics of animations

- Add an animation to the fighter plane when it moves

- Add text to the game to display the player's remaining lives and add a Game Over overlay when the player runs out of lives

A Bit of Refactoring

The starting code for this chapter can be found here: `https://github.com/Apress/monogame-mastery/tree/master/chapter-10/start`.

The first thing we did before writing new code for this chapter was to reorganize the Content Pipeline. Having all the sounds and images located in the same root folder was getting a little messy. We have four types of assets: sprites, images, music, and sounds. We added a folder in the content manager for each one of these types and moved our assets to be in the correct folders as seen in Figure 10-2.

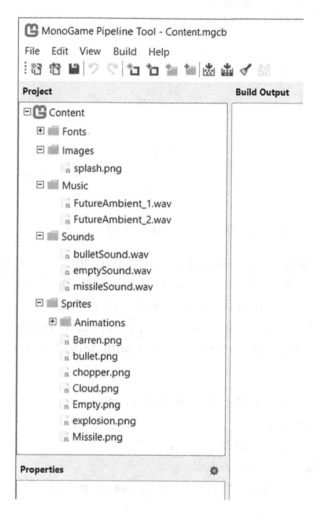

Figure 10-2. *Newly reorganized content pipeline*

You can ignore the Fonts and Animations folder for the moment since these will be added later in the chapter. To perform these changes, we first created actual directories on the hard disk within our Assets folder. See Figure 10-3.

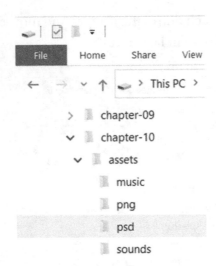

Figure 10-3. *New physical organization of assets*

We then opened the content pipeline xml file located at Content\
Content.mgcb within Visual Studio to edit the XML file directly because
the Content Pipeline user interface does not provide us with a way to move
assets around. For each one of our assets, we updated the location of the
physical asset and where it resides in the content pipeline. For example,
this

```
#begin ../../assets /FutureAmbient_1.wav
/importer:WavImporter
/processor:SoundEffectProcessor
/processorParam:Quality=Best
/build:../../assets/FutureAmbient_1.wav;FutureAmbient_1.wav
```

was updated with the correct file paths and content location:

```
#begin ../../assets/music/FutureAmbient_1.wav
/importer:WavImporter
/processor:SoundEffectProcessor
```

```
/processorParam:Quality=Best
/build:../../assets/music/FutureAmbient_1.wav;Music/
FutureAmbient_1.wav
```

We did this for all our assets, opened up the content pipeline user interface, and rebuilt our content pipeline to make sure we had no error. Finally, we now had to update the game code to load our sounds, music, and textures from their new location. For example:

```
public class GameplayState : BaseGameState
{
    private const string BackgroundTexture = "Sprites/Barren";
    private const string PlayerFighter = "Sprites/Animations/
    FighterSpriteSheet";
    private const string BulletTexture = "Sprites/bullet";
    private const string ExhaustTexture = "Sprites/Cloud";
    private const string MissileTexture = "Sprites/Missile";
    private const string ChopperTexture = "Sprites/Chopper";
    private const string ExplosionTexture = "Sprites/
    explosion";

    private const string TextFont = "Fonts/Lives";
    private const string GameOverFont = "Fonts/GameOver";

    private const string BulletSound = "Sounds/bulletSound";
    private const string MissileSound = "Sounds/missileSound";

    private const string Soundtrack1 = "Music/FutureAmbient_1";
    private const string Soundtrack2 = "Music/FutureAmbient_2";
}
```

Animations

2D animations are straightforward and follow the same principles that animators have used since the early twentieth century, where images are displayed in succession and rapidly enough to cause the illusion of movement. In two-dimensional games, programmers load multiple sprites in memory and tell the game to display them in sequence, one at a time, and control the speed of the animation by setting a frame count or time limit for each sprite.

Look at Figure 10-4 for all the sprites needed for the death animation of a skeleton character. By flipping through all those sprites, the skeleton comes to life… only to die.

Figure 10-4. *The death of a skeleton, one sprite at a time*

How fluid the animation looks depends on how many sprites are used and how long the animation lasts. With fewer frames, a faster animation is required to avoid any choppiness where the player can visibly notice each frame. However, such an effect may be desired in some games where, for example, the player character is idle and bobbing up and down. Just like the *Space Invaders* aliens, that idle character could require only two sprites: one for the bottom of the bob animation and one for the top.

Sprite Sheets

If we were to include the dying skeleton from Figure 10-4 into our game and animate it, would we have to add seven sprites to the content pipeline, name them, and load them in our game? Thankfully no, as that would be a lot of work, because this is just one animate, where the skeleton faces right.

A game could have skeletons facing left, up, and down, each with their own animations, adding up to 28 sprites in total! Instead, game developers use sprite sheets, which are just like our regular texture files, but with all the required game animation sprites in the same file, with usually one row per animation. A single sprite sheet covering all the animations required for our skeleton could then have a row for each of the following:

- Idle facing left

- Idle facing right

- Idle facing up

- Idle facing down

- Walking left

- Walking right

- Walking up

- Walking down

- Dying while facing left

- Dying while facing right

- Dying while facing up

- Dying while facing down

An artist would create all those sprites and place them into the sprite sheet file and provide the game developer with the dimensions of each sprite. With that information, we can then compute the location of any sprite within the sprite sheet. See Figure 10-5 for an example of a larger sprite sheet containing multiple animations. In this case, each row has one type of game character and multiple animations are on the same line. This sprite sheet comes from the open game arts website located here: https://opengameart.org/content/a-platformer-in-the-forest.

On that web page, we can see that the artist has written instructions for finding the sprites needed for different animations.

Figure 10-5. *Large sprite sheet with sprites for many animations, for many characters*

Texture Atlas

Texture atlases are similar to sprite sheets and we want to cover them briefly here because the two are sometimes mixed up. The principle is the same: build a single image file that contains multiple textures. The main difference between a sprite sheet and an atlas is that the atlas is typically not used for animations. Instead, it will contain textures needed for the game in general. See Figure 10-6 for an example of an atlas. Figure 10-7 shows how the atlas is used to build up a world.

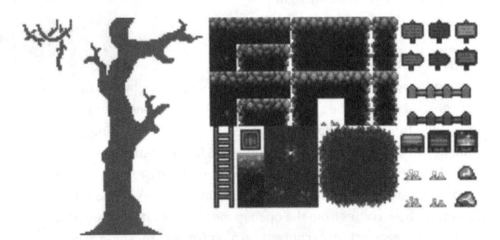

Figure 10-6. *A game atlas*

Figure 10-7. *Using an atlas to build a world*

Animation Downsides

When I play combat-style video games like *NieR:Automata*, *The Witcher 3*, or *Monster Hunter: World*, I prefer playing a quick and responsive combat style. These games all offer the player a choice between slow and powerful weapons, or quick and weaker weapons that hit for less damage than their heavy counterparts, but hit more often, resulting in similar damage over time. Every time I pick up a heavy weapon in those games and hit the attack button, I have to watch a weapon swing animation that takes a long time to complete. My character takes a step back, starts swinging their weapon around them, and then commits with all their might to crashing the weapon down on the target. Sometimes the animation takes a full three seconds, which feels like an eternity, and I cannot do anything else during that time.

245

Those long animations bring into light one of the downsides of the technique. It can be hard to fluidly move out of an animation in a video game because it is hard for designers to create different abilities and movement types in a way where they can be mixed and matched. What if halfway through a long sword swing, I decide to start running backward? In real life that could be doable: let the sword momentum turn me around while I bring the sword closer to my body and finally sheath it and start running. However, in a video game, game designers will rarely account for sudden change in movement, so players are forbidden from doing anything of the sort. You cannot cancel a sword swing, the same way that you cannot unsheathe a sword until it is fully sheathed. Doing so would force the unsheathing animation to start from the start while halfway through the sheathing animation, causing the sword to "jump" down in one frame, breaking the illusion of movement.

It is much easier to design a game if animations are forced to go to completion or if cancelling an animation to replace it with another does not cause anything weird visually.

State Machines

State machines are a useful way to manage, among other things,[1] the animations of game objects. We will not be using state machines in our game, but we thought it would be nice to mention them as they are a useful tool to help control and organize the complexity of managing the many possible states of game objects. For example, while hanging off the edge of a building in *Assassin's Creed*, the player cannot just start walking. First, they must either let go and fall or climb up the ledge and stand up

---

[1]Another use of state machines would be managing what to do with player commands. For example, pressing the down arrow could mean moving the character downward or dropping an item, depending on which state the character is in.

on the roof. We could add code like this in our gameplay state class and micromanage the player game object:

```
if (cmd is GameplayInputCommand.MoveUp && !player.IsHanging &&
    !player.IsFalling && !player.IsDead)
{
    player.MoveUp();
}
Else if (cmd is GameplayInputCommand.MoveUp && player.IsHanging
&& !player.IsDead)
{
    player.Climb();
}
```

However, as the game grows, managing all the different ways a player can move and interact with the world becomes complex and difficult to reason about. This is where state machines can help. A state machine is a collection of states that are connected to each other with directed edges. If state A has an edge that goes toward state B, it means we can transition from A to B. However, if state B does not have its own edge toward state A, we cannot transition back.

If we look at our previous example of an *Assassin's Creed* player hanging on a ledge, we could see the graph of states and edges depicted in Figure 10-8. That state machine has five different states and things start with the player initially in the idle state. From there, the player can only start walking, after which they can hang off a ledge or fall. When hanging, they can climb up or fall.

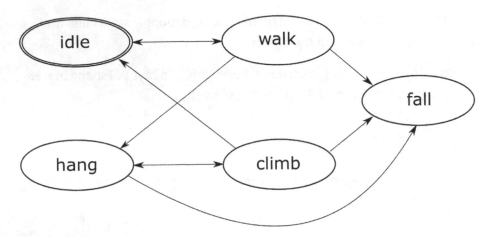

Figure 10-8. *A simple state machine*

Each state in our state machine has its own associated animation, so when it comes time to draw out our animations, the gameplay state simply has to ask the player game object to draw its current state's animation without having to care about the details of the game.

While we will not implement a state machine in our game, we thought it could be worth bringing up the technique because it is widely used in gaming. Should you decide to build a game using Unity one day, you will have to use state machines and associate states to animations.

Animation Engine

Any game object should only have a single active animation at a time, or no active animation while displaying a regular nonmoving sprite, which they can already do. Our strategy for implementing animations to our engine will be to add two classes: AnimationFrame and Animation, and let game objects manage their own animations. While it would be useful to add a state machine to the engine, we will not need this extra complexity for the simple animations found in vertical shooter games.

Let's start with the simplest of the two classes: the AnimationFrame. Its purpose is to hold information about each frame of an animation:

- Where its sprite is on a sprite sheet. We will use a Rectangle to store this into the class to make it easier when we later draw the sprite because the SpriteBatch. Draw method requires Rectangles.

- How long should this frame last, in number of frames.

Some animation engines calculate the length of each animation frames in seconds, which is useful when working with a framework that does not guarantee a fixed number of frames per seconds. In our case, MonoGame defaults to displaying 60 frames per second so we can easily reason about our animations in terms of number of frames. It is important to note, however, that this is just the default value. Some games run purposefully at 30 frames per second, in which case the animation frame lengths need to be updated so they run as fast as the 60 frames per second games. In other cases, slow gaming hardware could prevent MonoGame from operating at its desired update speed. In that case, animations that are measured using time instead of frames will keep operating at the same speed and may skip animation frames, while animations like ours that are using a frame count will appear to be slower.

Create an AnimationFrame class in the Engine\Objects\Animations directory:

```
public class AnimationFrame
{
    public Rectangle SourceRectangle { get; private set; }
    public int Lifespan { get; private set; }
```

```
    public AnimationFrame(Rectangle sourceRectangle, int
    lifespan)
    {
        SourceRectangle = sourceRectangle;
        Lifespan = lifespan;
    }
}
```

Now, let's start working on our Animation class, which is a little more complex. It will hold a list of animation frames and be able to tell our game which animation sprite needs to be drawn at any time given the age of the animation. It must also know whether an animation is looping or not. For example, and idle character bobbing up and down will use a looping animation, while a character climbing up a ledge will not use a looping animation. Finally, we should be able to reset an animation and bring it back to frame number 1, and the ability to create a reversed copy of an animation can be a neat utility.

Create an Animation class in the Engine\Objects\Animations directory, with the following class variables:

```
public class Animation
{
    private List<AnimationFrame> _frames = new
        List<AnimationFrame>();
    private int _animationAge = 0;
    private int _lifespan = -1;
    private bool _isLoop = false;
}
```

Here we have the _frames list of animation frames, the age of the animation, and whether the animation is a loop. We also have _lifespan, which will be used to hold the total length of the animation, in number of frames. It is calculated like this:

```
public int Lifespan {
    get
    {
        if (_lifespan < 0)
        {
            _lifespan = 0;
            foreach (var frame in _frames)
            {
                _lifespan += frame.Lifespan;
            }
        }
        return _lifespan;
    }
}
```

This property takes the sum of all the animation frames' lifespans and caches it in _lifespan before returning it. We can cache that value because once an animation is created, it will never change.

Getting the current frame of the animation is the core of this class. The algorithm works this way:

We will iterate through the frames of the animation and add their age into an accumulator variable. As we visit each frame, if the current age of the animation is smaller than the accumulator plus the current frame's lifespan, then we have found our current frame and return it. Otherwise, increment the accumulator by the current frame's lifespan and move on to the next frame. If, after iterating through all our frame, we still have not found our current frame, we will simply return the last one.

Figure 10-9 shows us a simple example of an animation with four frames, each one lasting 20 frames. If our animation's age is currently 35, then to compute our current frame we need to go through our algorithm.

- Frame 1: Accumulator = 0, so our animation age of 35 is not smaller than accumulator + 20. Next!

- Frame 2: Accumulator is now 20, which means that the animation age of 35 is smaller than accumulator + 20. We found our frame! Return frame number 2.

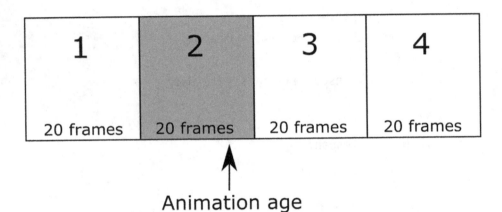

Figure 10-9. *Computing an animation's current frame based on the animation age*

The code that implements this algorithm is as follows:

```
public AnimationFrame CurrentFrame
{
    get
    {
        AnimationFrame currentFrame = null;

        var framesLifespan = 0;
        foreach (var frame in _frames)
```

```
    {
        if (framesLifespan + frame.Lifespan >=
            _animationAge)
        {
            currentFrame = frame;
            break;
        }
        else
        {
            framesLifespan += frame.Lifespan;
        }
    }

    if (currentFrame == null)
    {
        currentFrame = _frames.LastOrDefault();
    }

    return currentFrame;
    }
}
```

When creating an instance of the Animation class, we want to indicate whether this is a looping animation:

```
public Animation(bool looping)
{
    _isLoop = looping;
}
```

Then, our game objects, which will soon use our new animation class, can add frames to the animation one by one using the AddFrame method, by specifying the rectangle on the sprite sheet that corresponds to the frame that is being added, and the lifespan of the frame:

```
public void AddFrame(Rectangle sourceRectangle, int lifespan)
{
    _frames.Add(new AnimationFrame(sourceRectangle, lifespan));
}
```

Finally, we need to increment the age of the animation at each update. We also need to be able to reset the animation by setting its age back to zero.

```
public void Update(GameTime gametime)
{
    _animationAge++;

    if (_isLoop && _animationAge > Lifespan)
    {
        _animationAge = 0;
    }
}

public void Reset()
{
    _animationAge = 0;
}
```

Notice that in the case of a looping animation, when we increment the age during the Update method, we reset the age if the animation age is longer than its total lifespan, causing to start over.

Finally, we will add our utility function to reverse an animation, which returns a new animation with a reversed list of frames. This will be useful later.

```
public Animation ReverseAnimation
{
    get
    {
        var newAnimation = new Animation(_isLoop);
        for (int i = _frames.Count - 1; i >= 0; i--)
        {
            newAnimation.AddFrame(_frames[i].SourceRectangle,
            _frames[i].Lifespan);
        }

        return newAnimation;
    }
}
```

Animating Our Fighter Plane

We are now ready to add animations to the game and we think the fighter plane could use some polishing when it moves left or right. In real life, when a fighter jet moves sideways, it starts by tilting toward that direction, causing it to move that way. It would look interesting for our player sprite to tilt in the same manner while it moves around the bottom of the screen, so we created a sprite sheet with a few tilting increments in both directions. Figure 10-10 shows the sprite sheet that we created. However, instead of creating two rows for the left and right animations, they are all on the same row.

Figure 10-10. *All the frames of our moving fighter plane*

The sprite sheet is in the assets\png directory on the disk. Open up the Content Pipeline tool and add an Animations folder inside the Sprites folder. Inside the Animations folder, add a link to our fighter sprite sheet and call it FighterSpriteSheet.png. Save and build the content pipeline.

Open the PlayerSprite class in Visual Studio and add the following private variables:

```
private Animation _turnLeftAnimation = new Animation(false);
private Animation _turnRightAnimation = new Animation(false);
private Animation _leftToCenterAnimation = new Animation(false);
private Animation _rightToCenterAnimation = new Animation(false);
private const int AnimationSpeed = 3;
private const int AnimationCellWidth = 116;
private const int AnimationCellHeight= 152;

private Animation _currentAnimation;
private Rectangle _idleRectangle;

private bool _movingLeft = false;
private bool _movingRight = false;
```

Here we are adding a few animations to the game object. Our fighter jet tilts to the left or tilts to the right. It can also come back to center when the player stops moving. We are also defining a few values that we will use later. The tilting animation has a speed of 3, which we will use as the lifespan of each animation frame later. This is extremely fast! However, anything slower felt too choppy, so we opted for a fast animation instead of an animation with more intermediate frames.

Our private variables also track the height and width of each animation sprite on the sprite sheet. Finally, we track which animation is currently being played, which sprite is the idle sprite in the sprite sheet, and if the player is currently moving left or right. Let's now create our animations. Go to the PlayerSprite constructor and add the following code:

```
_idleRectangle = new Rectangle(348, 0, AnimationCellWidth,
    AnimationCellHeight);
_turnLeftAnimation.AddFrame(new Rectangle(348, 0,
    AnimationCellWidth, AnimationCellHeight),
    AnimationSpeed);
_turnLeftAnimation.AddFrame(new Rectangle(232, 0,
    AnimationCellWidth, AnimationCellHeight),
    AnimationSpeed);
_turnLeftAnimation.AddFrame(new Rectangle(116, 0,
    AnimationCellWidth, AnimationCellHeight),
    AnimationSpeed);
_turnLeftAnimation.AddFrame(new Rectangle(0,    0,
    AnimationCellWidth, AnimationCellHeight),
    AnimationSpeed);

_turnRightAnimation.AddFrame(new Rectangle(348, 0,
    AnimationCellWidth, AnimationCellHeight),
    AnimationSpeed);
_turnRightAnimation.AddFrame(new Rectangle(464, 0,
    AnimationCellWidth, AnimationCellHeight),
    AnimationSpeed);
_turnRightAnimation.AddFrame(new Rectangle(580, 0,
    AnimationCellWidth, AnimationCellHeight),
    AnimationSpeed);
```

```
_turnRightAnimation.AddFrame(new Rectangle(696, 0,
    AnimationCellWidth, AnimationCellHeight),
    AnimationSpeed);

_leftToCenterAnimation = _turnLeftAnimation.ReverseAnimation;
_rightToCenterAnimation = _turnRightAnimation.ReverseAnimation;
```

The preceding code sets the idle rectangle, representing the fighter plane in its idle state, which is the fourth sprite in our sprite sheet. The coordinates in the rectangle correspond to exactly the location of the sprite on the sprite sheet. We then create the _turnLeftAnimation by adding first four sprites in the sprite sheet. This is followed by creating the _turnRightAnimation, which adds the last four sprites in the sprite sheet.

Finally, to create the animations to return the plane to its idle position, we simply reverse the two animations that we created. We now have a total of four animations for our fighter jet. Let's use them!

Our PlayerSprite object already has a MoveLeft() and MoveRight() methods to change the position of the plane in the game. We will reuse those methods to also change the current animation of the object. We will also add a StopMoving() method to be able to play the appropriate reversed animation.

```
public void StopMoving()
{
    if (_movingLeft)
    {
        _currentAnimation = _leftToCenterAnimation;
        _movingLeft = false;
    }

    if (_movingRight)
    {
        _currentAnimation = _rightToCenterAnimation;
```

```
            _movingRight = false;
    }
}
public void MoveLeft()
{
    _movingLeft = true;
    _movingRight = false;
    _currentAnimation = _turnLeftAnimation;
    _leftToCenterAnimation.Reset();
    _turnRightAnimation.Reset();
    Position = new Vector2(Position.X - PlayerSpeed, Position.Y);
}

public void MoveRight()
{
    _movingRight = true;
    _movingLeft = false;
    _currentAnimation = _turnRightAnimation;
    _rightToCenterAnimation.Reset();
    _turnLeftAnimation.Reset();
    Position = new Vector2(Position.X + PlayerSpeed, Position.Y);
}
```

A few things are happening in MoveRight(). First, we set the _movingRight and _movingLeft Boolean variables accordingly so our object knows it is currently moving right. Then, we set the _currentAnimation to the _turnRightAnimation. Since we know we are not using the other animations at the moment, we reset them so they can be reused later. Finally, we update the position of the object on the screen. The MoveLeft() method works in a similar way.

The StopMoving() method, however, needs to know which way the plane was turning so it can bring it back to center. If it was moving left, then we use the _leftToCenterAnimation. Otherwise, we use the _rightToCenterAnimation. Finally, since we are not moving anymore, we reset both movement Boolean variables.

This is quite a bit of state tracking, but it is still manageable. However, if we started adding more functionality to our fighter game object, like moving vertically, we may have to think about using a state machine instead.

Only a few things are left for our new fighter plane to be usable. We need an Update() method so we can increase the age of the current animation, and we also need to find the current animation's frame so we can draw it. Or, if there is no current animation because the player stopped moving, we draw the idle sprite.

```
public void Update(GameTime gametime)
{
    if (_currentAnimation != null)
    {
        _currentAnimation.Update(gametime);
    }
}

public override void Render(SpriteBatch spriteBatch)
{
    var destinationRectangle =
        new Rectangle((int)_position.X, (int)_position.Y,
                        AnimationCellWidth, AnimationCellHeight);
    var sourceRectangle = _idleRectangle;
    if (_currentAnimation != null)
    {
        var currentFrame = _currentAnimation.CurrentFrame;
        if (currentFrame != null)
```

```
    {
        sourceRectangle = currentFrame.SourceRectangle;
    }
}

spriteBatch.Draw(_texture, destinationRectangle,
sourceRectangle, Color.White);
}
```

And there we have it. You can play with this new FighterSprite class in the DevState class and see how it performs when turning left and right.

The GameplayState class was modified to take into account a new GameplayInputCommand:

```
public class PlayerStopsMoving : GameplayInputCommand { }
```

This command is issued when the player is not pressing the left or right arrow keys in our input mapper, which was modified to this effect:

```
if (state.IsKeyDown(Keys.Right))
{
    commands.Add(new GameplayInputCommand.PlayerMoveRight());
}
else if (state.IsKeyDown(Keys.Left))
{
    commands.Add(new GameplayInputCommand.PlayerMoveLeft());
}
else
{
    commands.Add(new GameplayInputCommand.PlayerStopsMoving());
}
```

With that in place, the HandleInput() method in the GameplayState class can monitor for this command and react appropriately:

```
if (cmd is GameplayInputCommand.PlayerStopsMoving &&
!_playerDead)
{
    _playerSprite.StopMoving();
}
```

Finally, the GameplayState's UpdateGameState() method must call the Update() method on the PlayerSprite class. This is done with this simple call:

```
_playerSprite.Update(gameTime);
```

Text

Text is a major part of games everywhere. It is used for different purposes, like displaying the player score, a letter received by a player in an MMO, or a menu on the screen to let the player change their graphic settings. We will use text in our game to tell the player how many lives they have left and give them a Game Over screen when they run out of lives.

Fonts

To display text on the screen, you need sprites. Thankfully, we do not have to create our own sprite atlases that comprise all the font characters we need for our game. MonoGame takes care of this for us by rasterizing fonts that we already have on our computers. If you can use a particular font while editing text in a Word document, then that font is available for MonoGame, which will be happy to create font sprites for you.

Adding Fonts to the Content Pipeline

Creating font sprites for our game is fairly straightforward. We will use the Content Pipeline tool to add our game fonts, but we will need one extra step in order to correctly build our fonts. Open the Content Pipeline Tool and add a Fonts folder under Contents. As shown in Figure 10-11, in the Fonts folder, create two new items and select the SpriteFont Description option. Call each item GameOver and Lives. The reason we need two different fonts is that the game over text will be bigger than the live text, so we need to rasterize the two fonts independently into two different sprite fonts. Note that another sprite font option exists in the content pipeline for localized text. This is used when games are sold internationally, and text needs to change depending on the region of the world where the player lives. We will not cover this scenario in this chapter.

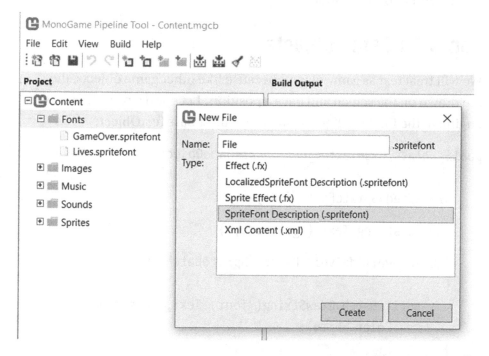

Figure 10-11. *Adding SpriteFonts to the content pipeline*

Save the content pipeline, but do not yet close the window. We have just created two files in our game solution, located in Content\Fonts\ called GameOver.spritefont and Lives.spritefont. Open both files in Visual Studio. As you can see, both files are also XML files and can be edited. In the Lives.spritefont, notice how the font is set to Arial on line 14:

```
<FontName>Arial</FontName>
```

Feel free to experiment with different fonts, but we decided to use the default font for the moment. However, we need to change the font size to 14 by changing this line in the file:

```
<Size>14</Size>
```

Save the file and open GameOver.spritefont and change the font size in that file to 50, and then save and close both files. You can now run a build in the content pipeline tool.

Fonts As Game Objects

We will treat text as game objects because like other game objects, they are drawn on the screen and have a position. Let's add a new class to our engine in the Engine\Objects directory called BaseTextObject:

```
public class BaseTextObject : BaseGameObject
{
    protected SpriteFont _font;

    public string Text { get; set; }

    public override void Render(SpriteBatch spriteBatch)
    {
        spriteBatch.DrawString(_font, Text, _position,
            Color.White);
    }
}
```

This class inherits from BaseGameObject, giving it all functionality of a GameObject, but we will ignore the _texture private variable in the base class. Instead, we will keep track of the sprite font used by each text object, and we provide a default rendering method that uses a new SpriteBatch method called DrawString(), which is used to draw text using a sprite font, a string, and a position.

Let's add our two text objects to our game. Add two classes in the Objects\Text directory – GameOverText and LivesText:

```
public class GameOverText : BaseTextObject
{
    public GameOverText(SpriteFont font)
    {
        _font = font;
        Text = "Game Over";
    }
}

public class LivesText : BaseTextObject
{
    private int _nbLives = -1;

    public int NbLives {
        get
        {
            return _nbLives;
        }
        set
        {
            _nbLives = value;
            Text = $"Lives: {_nbLives}";
        }
    }
```

```
    public LivesText(SpriteFont font)
    {
        _font = font;
    }
}
```

The GameOverText class is very straightforward and holds the "Game Over" text.

The LivesText class, on the other hand, has the extra responsibility of updating its text based on the number of remaining lives of the player. When the player loses a life, the GameplayState will set the NbLives property, which will cause the text being displayed to be updated.

Tracking Lives

Let's now track our player's lives. When the game starts, our player will have three lives. Add these private variables to the GameplayState class:

```
private const int StartingPlayerLives = 3;
private int _playerLives = StartingPlayerLives;
private const string TextFont = "Fonts/Lives";
private const string GameOverFont = "Fonts/GameOver";
private LivesText _livesText;
```

Here, we store our starting amount of lives, our sprite font locations, and an instance of the LivesText class, which is instantiated in the LoadContent() method:

```
_livesText = new LivesText(LoadFont(TextFont));
_livesText.NbLives = StartingPlayerLives;
_livesText.Position = new Vector2(10.0f, 690.0f);
AddGameObject(_livesText);
```

The preceding code uses a new LoadFont() function that was added to the BaseGameState class, which uses the content manager's Load function for SpriteFont classes:

```
protected SpriteFont LoadFont(string fontName)
{
    return _contentManager.Load<SpriteFont>(fontName);
}
```

With those elements in play and our LivesText text object being drawn, we are ready to lower the amount of lives whenever the KillPlayer() method is called:

```
_playerLives -= 1;
_livesText.NbLives = _playerLives;
if (_playerLives > 0)
{
    ResetGame();
}
else
{
    GameOver();
}
```

That code reduces _playerLives by one and updates the number of lives on the _livesText object. If that number is above zero, we reset the game. Otherwise, we call the GameOver() method, which we will implement shortly.

Game Over

We could just display a big "Game Over" text in the middle of the screen when the player runs out of lives, but that is a little bit boring so we will add an extra touch and also darken the screen a little to truly bring home the

point that the game is indeed over. First, let's implement the GameOver()
method. Start by adding this private variable to the GameplayState class to
track whether we are game over or not:

```
private bool _gameOver = false;
```

Then add the GameOver() method:

```
private void GameOver()
{
    var font = LoadFont(GameOverFont);
    var gameOverText = new GameOverText(font);
    var textPositionOnScreen = new Vector2(460, 300);

    gameOverText.Position = textPositionOnScreen;
    AddGameObject(gameOverText);
    _gameOver = true;
}
```

Similarly to how we add the LivesText object to the game, we load
the GameOver font and instantiate a GameOverText object that is then
positioned in the center of the screen before being added to the active
game objects. Finally, we set the _gameOver variable to true, which will
enable us to darken the screen.

The chosen strategy to darken the screen a bit is to draw a big
rectangle that fills the viewport using a black color and a 30% transparency
setting. To do this, we will override the BaseGameState's Render()
method and draw our game objects ourselves, after which we'll draw the
semitransparent dark rectangle to achieve our desired effect if we are game
over. First, change the BaseGameState's Render() method to be virtual so it
can be overridden:

```
public virtual void Render(SpriteBatch spriteBatch)
```

Then add the following code to the GameplayState class:

```
public override void Render(SpriteBatch spriteBatch)
{
    base.Render(spriteBatch);

    if (_gameOver)
    {
        // Draw black rectangle at 30% transparency
        var screenBoxTexture = GetScreenBoxTexture(spriteBatch.
        GraphicsDevice);
        var viewportRectangle = new Rectangle(0, 0,
        _viewportWidth, _viewportHeight);
        spriteBatch.Draw(screenBoxTexture, viewportRectangle,
        Color.Black * 0.3f);
    }
}

private Texture2D GetScreenBoxTexture(GraphicsDevice
graphicsDevice)
{
    if (_screenBoxTexture == null)
    {
        _screenBoxTexture = new Texture2D(graphicsDevice, 1, 1);
        _screenBoxTexture.SetData<Color>(new Color[] { Color.
        White });
    }

    return _screenBoxTexture;
}
```

The GameplayState's Render() method starts by calling the base class method that we are overriding. That takes care of drawing all the active game objects to the screen. Then, if we are game over, we create a blank texture that we cache for future use. The texture is white but it is quickly changed to a semitransparent black in the spriteBatch.Draw() function by multiplying the Color.Black value by 0.3.

Now, when the player loses three lives, the screen darkens, the game over text is displayed, and the game is allowed to keep running, without a fighter jet, until the player presses the escape key to exit the game.

Summary

In this chapter, we introduce our readers to how MonoGame handles text, enabling the display of information on the screen and opening up future possibilities like having a pause screen and menu screens. We also tackled 2D animations and how to add them to our game while taking some time to learn about state machines.

We believe that at this point in the book, you have all the tools that you need to start creating games. But as you may have noticed in this journey, some aspects of game programing are tedious. We also do not have a complete game right now. What is missing at this point is a proper level to play through.

In the next chapter, we will look at external game tools that can help speed up game design. We will also work on a level to play through and create a level editor to enable us to create future levels.

CHAPTER 11

Level Design

At this point in the book, you have all the tools that you need to start creating your own 2D games. But as you may have noticed in this journey, some aspects of game programming are tedious and the devil is in the details. Despite all our efforts so far, we still do not have a complete game, let alone a complete level to play through. All we have in the game is a player who has three attempts to destroy four helicopter enemies and then the background just keeps scrolling until the player quits the game. There is no challenge and no rewarding feeling.

In this chapter, you will

- – Design your own game level

- – Load a game level into the game

- – Add turrets as a new and very difficult enemy to deal with

Figure 11-1 is what you can expect the game to look like by the time we are done working through this chapter.

© Jarred Capellman, Louis Salin 2020
J. Capellman and L. Salin, *MonoGame Mastery*,
https://doi.org/10.1007/978-1-4842-6309-9_11

Figure 11-1. *Our end game*

As usual, you can find the code for the end of the chapter at `https://github.com/Apress/monogame-mastery/tree/master/chapter-11/end` and all the assets used in the game here: `https://github.com/Apress/monogame-mastery/tree/master/chapter-11/assets`.

Level Editors

Level editors are one of the most powerful tools for game design. With them, you can take the ideas that we implemented, the game mechanics and our game objects, and arrange them out on a level in a way that creates a challenge for the player and make the game fun to play.

You may have heard of what we think is the most popular level editor in the world right now: *Super Mario Maker*, which allows players around the world to design and build Super Mario levels that they can then upload on the Internet for other players to try.

In the early 1990s, one of the most popular games at the time was id Software's *Doom*, a classic first-person shooter that really made the whole genre mainstream. Shortly after its release, a Doom level editor was made available for download and thousands of Doom enthusiasts started creating their own levels, then playing through them.

Those editors were sophisticated. They provided users with a graphical user interface to build levels. With the Doom level editor, we spent hours connecting lines together to form walls and assigning properties to each wall to give it a texture or to mark doors. With Mario Maker, the player arranges game objects on a 2D level and can visually see what they are building as work. In the end, the game looks exactly like what the user sees in the editor. This requires a new level of effort that includes building a separate application (or an application within the game) to let users place down game objects in a what-you-see-is-what-you-get kind of way.

Our game, however, is not very complex. To design our levels, we can lay out enemies and obstacles in a grid-like pattern in a text document. While not as visual as the Doom level editor, we can still arrange things to make it easy to mentally visualize the player running through our design.

What Is a Level?

If we think about the kind of game we are building, it is a collection of background tiles placed on a grid with choppers being generated at certain times. We will later add turrets to the game, and they will be placed on the background tiles so organizing our level as a long vertical grid with the player starting at the bottom makes sense. When the game starts, it will read the first row of the grid, the one at the bottom, interpret it, and position things into play. It will then read the next row above it and position more things on the screen, and so on and so forth until it runs out of rows to read, at which point the player will have completed the level.

Look at this snippet of the level that we designed for the game in Figure 11-2. Imagine that the player sprite is in the middle at the bottom of the image and slowly moves upward. Each row of the grid has eleven elements: ten game object elements, followed by one last symbol that represents a global event. The full level text file can be found here: `https://github.com/Apress/monogame-mastery/blob/master/chapter-11/end/Levels/LevelData/Level1.txt`.

```
0,0,0,1,0,0,1,0,0,0,_
0,0,1,0,0,0,0,1,0,0,g2
0,0,0,0,0,0,0,0,0,0,_
0,0,0,0,0,0,0,0,0,0,g2
0,0,1,0,0,0,0,1,0,0,_
0,0,0,0,0,0,0,0,0,0,g2
0,1,0,0,0,0,0,0,0,0,_
0,0,0,0,0,0,0,0,0,0,g4
0,0,0,0,0,0,0,0,0,0,g2
0,0,0,0,0,0,0,0,0,0,_
0,0,0,0,0,0,0,0,0,0,g4
0,0,0,0,0,0,0,0,0,0,_
0,0,0,0,0,0,0,0,0,0,g2
0,0,0,0,0,0,0,0,0,0,s
```

Figure 11-2. *A snippet of a level, codified into text*

Our grid has rows of ten elements which represent game objects positioned on the screen. There is also an eleventh element at the end of each row to represent game-wide events like generating enemies. Look at the following legend for the meaning of each element:

- 0: Nothing is going on here. Do not add anything to the game in this area of the grid.

- 1: Add a turret in this location on the screen.

- _: This level row does not trigger any game event.

- gN: A "g" followed by a number will trigger the generation of N number of enemy choppers whenever this row gets evaluated by the game.

— s: Indicates the start of the level, allowing the game to later wish good luck to the player.

— e: Indicates the end of the level, allowing the game to later congratulate the player.

As each game level row is evaluated, the viewport will be divided into ten even grid sections. When the game evaluates that a turret needs to be placed, it will be placed just off the top of the screen in its proper horizontal location on the grid so it can slowly scroll down into play.

How fast should we execute each row? That is entirely up to the game designer, but we opted for a two-second reading speed. Our current level, as designed, has a total of 48 lines, so running through the entire level would take 96 seconds, which feels about right for the total length of play time required for this type of game.

This file can be edited at any time by the game designer. The number of choppers generated can be changed, or when they are generated can also be modified by replacing "gN" element with "_" to remove the generation of choppers at this row of the level. Similarly, "_" can be replaced by "gN" elements to add the generation of choppers. Moving turrets around is also easy by changing "0"s to "1"s on our grid. Whenever the game is recompiled and run, the newly edited level will be played by the game.

Level Events

As we read the level rows from the level text file, we will generate level events that any game state object can register for. We will have one event for each kind of situation described in the last section. Let's start adding some code! Create a Levels directory in the project and add a LevelEvents.cs file with the following code:

```
public class LevelEvents : BaseGameStateEvent
{
    public class GenerateEnemies : LevelEvents
    {
        public int NbEnemies { get; private set; }
        public GenerateEnemies(int nbEnemies)
        {
            NbEnemies = nbEnemies;
        }
    }

    public class GenerateTurret : LevelEvents
    {
        public float XPosition { get; private set; }
        public GenerateTurret(float xPosition)
        {
            XPosition = xPosition;
        }
    }

    public class StartLevel : LevelEvents { }
    public class EndLevel : LevelEvents { }
    public class NoRowEvent : LevelEvents { }
}
```

These events will be triggered by the Level class further down as it interprets each element of each row in our level grid. These events will allow us to generate any number of enemy choppers or to position turrets at a specific X coordinate above the viewport.

Level Readers, Levels, and Our Gameplay State

We need the ability to read our level text files, but before we do this, we should create our first level. You can either copy the level.txt file at the URL we specified earlier or create a new one for your own needs. Either way, put it in Levels\LevelData\Level1.txt and make sure it is added to the project in Visual Studio. Then, open the file's properties in Visual Studio and make sure the Build Action is set to Embedded Resource, as shown in Figure 11-3.

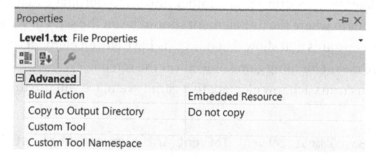

Figure 11-3. *Level1.txt is an embedded resource.*

Having our levels as an embedded resource is nice because the internal representation of our levels will not be directly available to users, who could go and edit the files themselves and potentially ruin the game by overwriting the original files with something that will either break the game or destroy the design of each level. By embedding the files, the levels become resources that are located into the executable file directly and much harder to access.

We can now add a LevelReader class responsible for loading the file and transforming it into a level grid. Add the class in the Levels directory:

```
public class LevelReader
{
    private int _viewportWidth;
```

```
    private const int NB_ROWS = 11;
    private const int NB_TILE_ROWS = 10;

    public LevelReader(int viewportWidth)
    {
        _viewportWidth = viewportWidth;
    }
}
```

We instantiate the class with a viewportWidth parameter that will be used later to transform a grid number into an X coordinate that corresponds to where the row element should be on the screen. We also have two constants that show that our grids have eleven elements, ten of which are meant for tiling game objects on the screen.

To transform each row element to a game event, we will use this function:

```
private BaseGameStateEvent ToEvent(int elementNumber, string
input)
{
    switch (input)
    {
        case "0":
            return new BaseGameStateEvent.Nothing();

        case "_":
            return new LevelEvents.NoRowEvent();

        case "1":
            var xPosition = elementNumber * _viewportWidth /
            NB_TILE_ROWS;
            return new LevelEvents.GenerateTurret(xPosition);

        case "s":
            return new LevelEvents.StartLevel();
```

```
        case "e":
            return new LevelEvents.EndLevel();

        case string g when g.StartsWith("g"):
            var nb = int.Parse(g.Substring(1));
            return new LevelEvents.GenerateEnemies(nb);

        default:
            return new BaseGameStateEvent.Nothing();
    }
}
```

The function takes the string that represents a single row element and the position of that element on the row. If it's a "0" or "_", we return the corresponding event to indicate that nothing is happening. The main reason to use two separate events here is to differentiate with nothing to add to the screen and a global event that can be used to cancel a previous global event. For example, the "s" start level event is cancelled when the next NoRowEvent is triggered. If our character is a "1", then we calculate the X coordinate of the current row element and pass it to the event. If our character is a "s" or an "e", then we trigger the StartLevel or EndLevel events. Finally, when the string starts with a "g", we read the rest of the string and convert it to an integer, which tells us how many choppers to create.

The next function will be responsible for iterating through each row and extracting all those level events from it. It will take a level string and split it by commas, then iterate over each element, and convert it to an event before returning a list of events for the entire row:

```
private List<BaseGameStateEvent> ToEventRow(string rowString)
{
    var elements = rowString.Split(',');
    var newRow = new List<BaseGameStateEvent>();
```

```
for (int i = 0; i < NB_ROWS; i++)
{
    newRow.Add(ToEvent(i, elements[i]));
}

return newRow;
}
```

Finally, we will add a public function that will load any level by its number by locating the embedded text file from within the assembly, reading it into memory and transforming it to a grid of level events.

```
public List<List<BaseGameStateEvent>> LoadLevel(int nb)
{
    var assembly = Assembly.GetExecutingAssembly();
    var assemblyName = assembly.FullName.Split(',')[0];
    var fileName = $"{assemblyName}.Levels.LevelData.Level{nb}.
    txt";

    var stream = assembly.GetManifestResourceStream(fileName);
    var reader = new StreamReader(stream);
    var levelString = reader.ReadToEnd();

    var rows = levelString.Split(Environment.NewLine.
        ToCharArray(), StringSplitOptions.RemoveEmptyEntries);
    var convertedRows = from r in rows
                        select ToEventRow(r);

    return convertedRows.Reverse().ToList();
}
```

Since the text file is read in memory top to bottom and we want to execute the level in the opposite direction, we reverse the list at the end so the events can be played out in the correct order.

We can now read level text files and convert them to a grid of level events. All that remains to be implemented now is the Level class, which will take in a level event grid and read each row of events every two seconds for our gameplay state. Create a Level class in the same directory we put our LevelReader and LevelEvents classes:

```
public class Level
{
    private LevelReader _levelReader;
    private List<List<BaseGameStateEvent>> _currentLevel;
    private int _currentLevelNumber;
    private int _currentLevelRow;

    private TimeSpan _startGameTime;
    private readonly TimeSpan TickTimeSpan = new TimeSpan(0,
        0, 2);

    public event EventHandler<LevelEvents.GenerateEnemies>
        OnGenerateEnemies;
    public event EventHandler<LevelEvents.GenerateTurret>
        OnGenerateTurret;
    public event EventHandler<LevelEvents.StartLevel>
        OnLevelStart;
    public event EventHandler<LevelEvents.EndLevel> OnLevelEnd;
    public event EventHandler<LevelEvents.NoRowEvent>
        OnLevelNoRowEvent;
```

```
    public Level(LevelReader reader)
    {
        _levelReader = reader;
        _currentLevelNumber = 1;
        _currentLevelRow = 0;

        _currentLevel = _levelReader.LoadLevel(
            _currentLevelNumber);
    }
}
```

The Level class has access to a level reader, which is passed in as a parameter via the constructor, which sets the initial current level number to 1 and the current level row to 0 and then uses the reader to load level 1. Most importantly, the constant TickTimeSpan is set to a time span of two seconds, which will be used further down to determine how long to wait until we can read the next row of level events.

The class also offers some utility functions, like resetting the level when the player dies or loading the next level for us:

```
public void LoadNextLevel()
{
    _currentLevelNumber++;
    _currentLevel = _levelReader.LoadLevel(
        _currentLevelNumber);
}

public void Reset()
{
    _currentLevelRow = 0;
}
```

Finally, the core method of the following class reads the level events of the current level row if two full seconds have passed. For each event, it triggers a .Net event that the gameplay state class will have registered to:

```
public void GenerateLevelEvents(GameTime gameTime)
{
    // Only generate events every 2 seconds
    if (_startGameTime == null)
    {
        _startGameTime = gameTime.TotalGameTime;
    }

    // Nothing to do until tick time
    if (gameTime.TotalGameTime - _startGameTime < TickTimeSpan)
    {
        return;
    }

    _startGameTime = gameTime.TotalGameTime;

    foreach (var e in _currentLevel[_currentLevelRow])
    {
        switch (e)
        {
            case LevelEvents.GenerateEnemies g:
                OnGenerateEnemies?.Invoke(this, g);
                break;

            case LevelEvents.GenerateTurret g:
                OnGenerateTurret?.Invoke(this, g);
                break;

            case LevelEvents.StartLevel s:
                OnLevelStart?.Invoke(this, s);
                break;
```

```
            case LevelEvents.EndLevel s:
                OnLevelEnd?.Invoke(this, s);
                break;

            case LevelEvents.NoRowEvent n:
                OnLevelNoRowEvent?.Invoke(this, n);
                break;
        }
    }

    _currentLevelRow++;
}
```

We are now ready to load our first level, although we will not handle turrets just yet. Open the GameplayState class and add a private variable for our level:

```
private Level _level;
```

Then update the LoadContent() method to create the level:

```
var levelReader = new LevelReader(_viewportWidth);
_level = new Level(levelReader);

_level.OnGenerateEnemies += _level_OnGenerateEnemies;
_level.OnGenerateTurret += _level_OnGenerateTurret;
_level.OnLevelStart += _level_OnLevelStart;
_level.OnLevelEnd += _level_OnLevelEnd;
_level.OnLevelNoRowEvent += _level_OnLevelNoRowEvent;
```

Let's now create each event handler that we used to register for the game events. We will leave most of them empty for the time being so we can focus on the proper execution of our levels. The only event we can handle is the one that generates enemies because we already have a chopper generator object, although we did need to refactor it so the same generator instance can be reused for different number of enemies.

```
private void _level_OnLevelStart(object sender,
LevelEvents.StartLevel e)
{
    // Left intentionally blank for now
}

private void _level_OnLevelEnd(object sender,
LevelEvents.EndLevel e)
{
    // Left intentionally blank for now
}

private void _level_OnLevelNoRowEvent(object sender,
LevelEvents.NoRowEvent e)
{
    // Left intentionally blank for now
}

private void _level_OnGenerateTurret(object sender,
LevelEvents.GenerateTurret e)
{
    // left intentionally blank for now
}
private void _level_OnGenerateEnemies(object sender,
LevelEvents.GenerateEnemies e)
{
    _chopperGenerator.GenerateChoppers(e.NbEnemies);
}
```

We will not cover the changes needed to update the chopper generator here. Feel free to look up the updated class in our GitHub repository or try to refactor it and see if you can match the way we called it earlier.

So that levels are run properly, we need to generate events at every update. Add this line to the UpdateGameState() method:

```
_level.GenerateLevelEvents(gameTime);
```

When the player dies, we need to reset the level so they can get a second or third chance at clearing it. Update the ResetGame() method and add this line at the bottom:

```
_level.Reset();
```

Run the game and see if it can read the level correctly and generate the number of chopper enemies you set on each level row!

Adding Turrets

Our game is not too challenging at the moment. Chopper enemies are generated and fly through the screen, but there are some safe spots in the bottom corners of the screen where the player sprite will never be hit by anything. To change this, we could add new chopper paths to the game, or we could add turrets that shoot at the player, wherever the player happens to be. This will eliminate any safe spot from the game but will introduce a new problem. Since the turrets are going to scroll down at the same speed as the background, they will eventually reach the bottom of the screen and be horizontally level with the player and shoot bullets that the player will not be able to avoid. To give the player a chance of surviving this situation, we must let the player move up and down! This is a simple functionality to add and only requires a few code changes. Let's see if you can do it on your own!

We made two other changes to the code. The first was to move the background scrolling speed out of the TerrainBackground class and into the GameplayState class so it can be shared with our turrets further down. The second change was to update the _onObjectChanged() event handler so it can handle any kind of BaseGameObject instead of just ChopperSprite objects.

Game Art and Origins

The game art for the new turrets has three sprites. A turret base (Tower. png), a double cannon (MG2.png), and a bullet sprite (Bullet_MG.pgn). These assets are in the Assets\png directory and just need to be added to the content pipeline under a new folder called Sprites\Turrets. We have kept their pipeline names the same.

The base and the cannon will need to be assembled on top of each other, with the cannon rotating over the base as it tracks the player. Look at Figure 11-4, which shows the cannon and the turret base sprites with their origin and the X and Y axis drawn over them. The white circles, located between the two gun barrels over its base, indicate the center of rotation of the cannon sprite. This is important to note because although the X coordinate of that center of rotation is exactly at half the width of the texture, its Y coordinate is not and is set to 158 pixels. The center of rotation is also called the origin of the image because all game objects will rotate around their origin, a subject that we briefly approached when making the helicopter blades spin in a previous chapter.

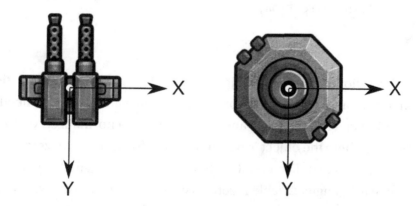

Figure 11-4. *The cannon part of the turret, with origin and X and Y axis*

Another important aspect of this cannon image is that unrotated, with an angle of zero degrees, it points up instead of toward the right. Because of this, it is important that we distinguish between the angle of our turret and the actual direction it is pointing to. Game objects are rarely fixed and will often rotate, so we should incorporate that into our BaseGameObject. Open up the class and add the following code:

```
public class BaseGameObject
{
    protected float _angle;
    protected Vector2 _direction;

    protected Vector2 CalculateDirection(
        float angleOffset = 0.0f)
    {
        _direction = new Vector2((float)Math.Cos(
            _angle - angleOffset),
            (float)Math.Sin(_angle - angleOffset));
        _direction.Normalize();
        return _direction;
    }
}
```

This will allow all our game objects to maintain an angle and direction that can be updated based on the protected _angle variable. When needed, a game object can use the angle and an offset to get a normalized vector representing where the object is pointing. The offset defaults to zero, in which case CalculateDirection() will return a vector aligned with the X axis when the _angle variable is zero as well. However, as we'll see in the following, our turret cannon points up instead of right when its angle is zero, so we'll provide an offset to get an accurate direction.

Let's create our TurretSprite class in the Objects\ directory and start by looking at its initialization:

```
public class TurretSprite : BaseGameObject
{
    private Texture2D _baseTexture;
    private Texture2D _cannonTexture;

    private float _moveSpeed;

    // With an angle of zero, the turret points up
    // so track offset for calculations when tracking player
    private const float AngleOffset = MathHelper.Pi / 2;
    private const float Scale = 0.3f;
    private const float AngleSpeed = 0.02f;
    private const int BulletsPerShot = 3;
    private const float CannonCenterPosY = 158;

    private int _hitAt = 100;
    private int _life = 50;

    private Vector2 _baseCenterPosition;
    private Vector2 _cannonCenterPosition;
    private float _baseTextureWidth;
    private float _baseTextureHeight;
    private bool _isShootingBullets;
    private TimeSpan _lastBulletShotAt;
    private int _bulletsRemaining;
    private bool _attackMode;

    public bool Active { get; set; }

    public event EventHandler<GameplayEvents.TurretShoots>
    OnTurretShoots;
```

```
public TurretSprite(Texture2D baseTexture, Texture2D
cannonTexture, float moveSpeed)
{
    _isShootingBullets = false;
    _moveSpeed = moveSpeed;
    _baseTexture = baseTexture;
    _cannonTexture = cannonTexture;
    _angle = MathHelper.Pi;  // point down by default
    _bulletsRemaining = BulletsPerShot;
    _attackMode = false;
    Active = false;

    _direction = CalculateDirection(AngleOffset);

    _baseTextureWidth = _baseTexture.Width * Scale;
    _baseTextureHeight = _baseTexture.Height * Scale;

    _baseCenterPosition = new Vector2(_baseTextureWidth /
        2f, _baseTextureHeight / 2f);
    _cannonCenterPosition = new Vector2(_cannonTexture.
        Width / 2f, CannonCenterPosY);

    AddBoundingBox(new Engine.Objects.BoundingBox(new
        Vector2(0, 0),
        _baseTexture.Width * Scale,
        _baseTexture.Height * Scale));
    }
}
```

Let's look at all those private variables one by one. First off, the turret must keep track of two textures for its base and its cannon since it will be responsible for handling both. Since this turret will be moving down at the same speed as the background, we need to know how fast it needs to go and we use the _moveSpeed variable for that.

Then we have a few constants to help shape the behavior of the turret. The angle offset is the angle between the X axis and the direction of the turret when _angle is equal to zero. We will use that to calculate the _direction vector whenever the cannon spins. The turret sprite image is also a little too big so we'll shrink it by a factor of 0.3. AngleSpeed is used to set how quickly the cannon can spin, and BulletsPerShots tells us how many bullets the turret will shoot in a single volley. Once it locates the player, it will stop moving and shoot three bullets. Because it stops moving, it gives the player a chance to dodge the bullets and reposition and ideally shoot the turret itself while it is busy shooting toward where the player used to be.

Let's talk angles now. The angle of the turret is set to MathHelper. Pi to force it to point down initially. That angle is set in radians, so PI represents a 180 degrees change, and since the initial image points up by default, the change causes it to flip and point down. This is purely a cosmetic thing. As the turret comes into view from the top of the screen, we feel like it looks nicer if it points down. Given this initial _angle value of 180 degrees, and given that pointing down in MonoGame means doing a clockwise rotation of 90 degrees, we have a discrepancy of 90 degrees between the object's angle and direction. To compensate, we set the AngleOffset constant to PI / 2, which is 90 degrees.

The _active Boolean variable is used to prevent the turret from spinning or attacking, since it wouldn't be very fun for turrets to attack the player while offscreen. Also, like our chopper enemy game object, our turrets can be attacked, so they have a certain amount of _life points. _hitAt is similarly initialized at a high number, just like the choppers, and is used in the Render() method to make the turret flash when hit.

Finally, we keep track of some coordinates and use _isShootingBullets, _lastBulletShotAt, _bulletsRemaining, and _attackMode to govern how quickly the turret is shooting, how many bullets remain in the current volley, or if the turret should move or shoot. The way the turret shoots is similar to how the gameplay state is controlling how often the player can shoot.

The TurretSprite constructor initializes all these private variables, taking into account the fact that our image is scaled down. It also adds a bounding box to the game object.

Every time our turret spins via these two utility functions, we recalculate the direction of the cannon, always taking the AngleOffset into consideration:

```
public void MoveLeft()
{
    _angle -= AngleSpeed;
    _direction = CalculateDirection(AngleOffset);
}

public void MoveRight()
{
    _angle += AngleSpeed;
    _direction = CalculateDirection(AngleOffset);
}
```

The only thing that will cause the cannon to rotate is the location of the player on the screen, so let's add an Update method to the TurretSprite class that takes a current player location and the game time as parameters:

```
public void Update(GameTime gameTime, Vector2 currentPlayerCenter)
{
    // Move turret down
    Position = Vector2.Add(_position, new Vector2(0,
    _moveSpeed));

    // If turret is not active, it cannot spin or shoot
    if (!Active)
    {
        return;
    }
```

```
// Can either attack and shoot 3 bullets or move. Not both
if (_attackMode && _bulletsRemaining > 0)
{
    Shoot(gameTime);
}
else
{
    var centerOfCannon = Vector2.Add(_position,
        _cannonCenterPosition * Scale);
    var playerVector = Vector2.Subtract(currentPlayerCenter,
        centerOfCannon);
    playerVector.Normalize();

    var angleTurret = Math.Atan2(_direction.Y,
        _direction.X);
    var anglePlayer = Math.Atan2(playerVector.Y,
        playerVector.X);
    var angleDiff = angleTurret - anglePlayer;

    var tolerance = 0.1f;
    if (angleDiff > tolerance)
    {
        MoveLeft();
    }
    else if (angleDiff < -tolerance)
    {
        MoveRight();
    }

    if (angleTurret >= anglePlayer - tolerance &&
    angleTurret <= anglePlayer + tolerance)
    {
        _attackMode = true;
```

```
            Shoot(gameTime);
        }
    }

    if (_bulletsRemaining <= 0)
    {
        _attackMode = false;
    }

    // Prevent firing bullets too quickly
    if (_lastBulletShotAt != null &&
        gameTime.TotalGameTime - _lastBulletShotAt >
        TimeSpan.FromSeconds(0.3))
    {
        _isShootingBullets = false;
    }

    // Reload bullets every 2 seconds
    if (gameTime.TotalGameTime - _lastBulletShotAt >
    TimeSpan.FromSeconds(2))
    {
        _bulletsRemaining = BulletsPerShot;
    }
}
```

A lot is happening here so we'll take some time to go through this step by step. First, we move the turret downward to help with the illusion that the player is flying upward. Whether the turret is inactive, shooting, or tracking the player, it must also move down to the bottom of the screen. Then, if the turret is inactive, we exit the method because we do not want to track or shoot the player until the turret is activated. Following that, we have two branches: the turret is shooting three bullets in a single direction, or it is spinning to get a lock on the player's center location. If the turret is in attack mode and has remaining bullets to shoot, it keeps shooting. Otherwise, it spins.

When spinning, the turret must determine where the player is in relation to itself. We pass in the player's sprite center location as a parameter to the Update() method, but before we can use it, we must transform it. Look at Figure 11-5 for an example. Vectors a and b denote the position of our turret and fighter jet objects on the screen. Because the Update() method belongs to the TurretSprite class, we have access to the b vector via the _position variable, and the player center position is passed in as a parameter to the method, which gives us the a vector. We have also been calculating the d vector, which is the direction of the turret, whenever the _angle variable changes. However, to determine if the turret points toward the player, we need to calculate the angle between the d vector and the c vector, which we do not currently have. But there is a simple solution to this.

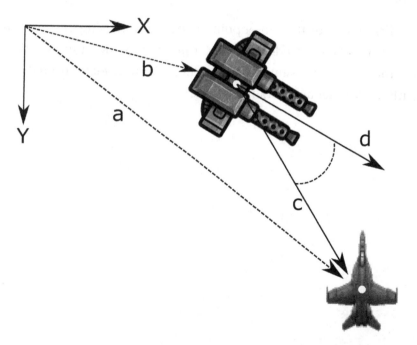

Figure 11-5. *Vectors and angles. Does the turret point toward the player?*

If we subtract the vector b from both object positions, we are essentially bringing the center of the turret back to the (0, 0) origin of the game screen. Because we are subtracting that b vector from the fighter plane position too, the plane will remain in the same location *relative to the turret*. This gives us a new way to think about the objects, as seen in Figure 11-6. Note that we are not actually moving the game objects on the screen, just manipulating variables for calculation purposes. Another way to think about this is that since a = b + c, then c = a – b. So, this is what these two lines do:

```
var centerOfCannon = Vector2.Add(_position,
_cannonCenterPosition * Scale);
var playerVector = Vector2.Subtract(currentPlayerCenter,
centerOfCannon);
```

The first line finds the center point of the cannon using the position of the object and the scaled-down center position of the cannon in the texture image. Then we subtract the centerOfCannon vector from the currentPlayerCenter and obtain our c vector.

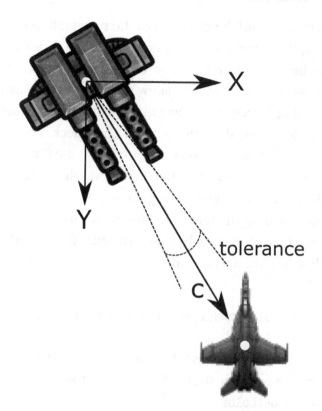

Figure 11-6. *The turret, located at the origin, points at the player object.*

Once we have the c vector, we can calculate its angle and the angle of the turret direction vector and then compare them to each other. If they fall within a certain tolerance area, we consider that the turret points at the player. The main reason for this tolerance zone is because as the turret spins, it may overshoot the player. Without any tolerance, the algorithm would then cause the turret to backtrack and overshoot the player again in the other direction, causing to change direction and so on, and so forth. The turret on the screen would appear blurry as it continuously spins up and down relentlessly. The tolerance zone lets it sit still and provides a much better visual effect. If the angle difference between c and the direction of the turret falls within this tolerance zone, the turret goes into attack mode and shoots.

Then, we check if the turret has any remaining bullets left. If it has none, we turn off the attack mode to allow the turret to spin again. Finally, we have two timing functions. The first one ensures that the turret cannot shoot bullets quicker than three per second. That check is very similar to how we prevent the player from shooting too fast in the GameplayState class. Finally, we want to make sure the turret gives the player a two-second break before it starts shooting again.

We now have to draw the turret on the screen, and because we are drawing two sprites on top of each other and because we want the turret to flash when shot, just like the helicopters, we will override the base class's Render() method:

```
public override void Render(SpriteBatch spriteBatch)
{
    // If the turret was just hit and is flashing, Color should
    // alternate between OrangeRed and White
    var color = GetColor();

    var cannonPosX = _position.X + _baseCenterPosition.X;
    var cannonPosY = _position.Y + _baseCenterPosition.Y;
    var cannonPosition = new Vector2(cannonPosX, cannonPosY);

    spriteBatch.Draw(_baseTexture, _position,
        _baseTexture.Bounds, color, 0, new Vector2(0, 0),
        Scale, SpriteEffects.None, 0f);
    spriteBatch.Draw(_cannonTexture, cannonPosition,
        _cannonTexture.Bounds, Color.White,
        _angle, _cannonCenterPosition, Scale,
        SpriteEffects.None, 0f);
}
```

The Render() method starts by finding the center location of the cannon. Then it draws the base of the turret without much fanfare. Finally, it draws the cannon and it gets a little bit more complicated. That second Draw() method is being used with a rotation angle, an origin vector, and a scale. This is what happens underneath the covers. MonoGame takes our texture and moves it so the (0, 0) origin is exactly where the _cannonCenterPosition is. Then it rotates the texture around the origin before moving it back to the cannonPosition.

The rest of the TurretSprite code like GetColor(), OnNotify(), and JustHit() are exactly the same as the ChopperSprite code, which we went over in collision detection chapter.

Turret Bullets

The last remaining item to have a fully functional turret is creating the bullets, which will be more complex than the bullets the player can shoot. This time, the turret bullets are a little bit more complex. Our fighter plane bullets were easy to implement because they move straight up the screen and have axis aligned bounding boxes for collision detection. The turret bullets, on the other hand, will most of the time move diagonally and cannot have axis aligned bounding boxes because that could cause collisions between the bullet and the plane even if they do not touch each other.

We need to determine where we want the bullets to be initially located on the screen, which is exactly behind the two barrels. We also want the bullets to also be angled and going toward the same direction as the turret. The turret is responsible for telling the gameplay state class, via the TurretShoots event, to create the actual game objects and will supply the angle and direction of the bullets to the state class. The Shoot() method is implemented as follows:

```
public void Shoot(GameTime gameTime)
{
```

```
if (!_isShootingBullets && _bulletsRemaining > 0)
{
    var centerOfCannon = Vector2.Add(_position,
    _baseCenterPosition);

    // Find perpendicular vectors to position bullets left
    // and right of the center of the cannon
    var perpendicularClockwiseDirection = new Vector2(
    _direction.Y, -_direction.X);
    var perpendicularCounterClockwiseDirection = new
    Vector2(-_direction.Y, _direction.X);

    var bullet1Pos =
        Vector2.Add(centerOfCannon,
        perpendicularClockwiseDirection * 10);
    var bullet2Pos =
        Vector2.Add(centerOfCannon,
        perpendicularCounterClockwiseDirection * 10);

    var bulletInfo =
        new GameplayEvents.TurretShoots(bullet1Pos,
        bullet2Pos, _angle, _direction);

    _bulletsRemaining--;
    _isShootingBullets = true;
    _lastBulletShotAt = gameTime.TotalGameTime;

    OnTurretShoots?.Invoke(this, bulletInfo);
}
}
```

First, we check if the we are allowed to shoot another round of bullets. The _isShootingBullets is set to true by the Update() method when we first start shooting, but will not be false until 0.3 seconds have passed by. We also need to have some bullets remaining. If those two conditions are met, then we can start the bullet object creation process. We need to find two vectors that are perpendicular to the turret's current direction and opposing each other, as seen in Figure 11-7. That will be the starting position of the bullets b1 and b2. Once we have those two vectors, which are normalized because they are calculated from the direction vector, which is also normalized, we multiply them by 10. A normalized vector has a length of one, so to be useful, that vector needs to be a bit longer here and 10 seems to be just the right number to move the bullets away from the center of the cannon and under the barrels.

Figure 11-7. *The initial location of the two turret bullets b1 and b2*

Let's add the TurretShoots game event to the GameplayEvents class:

```
public class TurretShoots : GameplayEvents
{
    public Vector2 Direction { get; private set; }
    public Vector2 Bullet1Position { get; private set; }
    public Vector2 Bullet2Position { get; private set; }
    public float Angle { get; private set; }
```

```
    public TurretShoots(Vector2 bullet1Pos, Vector2 bullet2Pos,
                        float angle, Vector2 direction)
    {
        Direction = direction;
        Bullet1Position = bullet1Pos;
        Bullet2Position = bullet2Pos;
        Angle = angle;
    }
}
```

Now we need to change the GameplayClass so it does something with that event. While we are in the class, let's add the code needed to create game turrets as well:

```
public class GameplayState : BaseGameState
{
    private const string TurretTexture = "Sprites/Turrets/Tower";
    private const string TurretMG2Texture = "Sprites/Turrets/MG2";
    private const string TurretBulletTexture = "Sprites/Turrets/
    Bullet_MG";

    private List<TurretSprite> _turretList = new
    List<TurretSprite>();
    private List<TurretBulletSprite> _turretBulletList = new
    List<TurretBulletSprite>();

    private void _level_OnGenerateTurret(object sender,
    LevelEvents.GenerateTurret e)
    {
        var turret = new TurretSprite(LoadTexture(TurretTexture),
                                      LoadTexture(TurretMG2
                                      Texture),
                                      SCOLLING_SPEED);
```

```
    // Position the turret offscreen at the top
    turret.Position = new Vector2(e.XPosition, -100);

    turret.OnTurretShoots += _turret_OnTurretShoots;
    turret.OnObjectChanged += _onObjectChanged;
    AddGameObject(turret);

    _turretList.Add(turret);
  }
}
```

This code creates empty lists of turrets and turret bullets that we will keep track of over time and implements the _level_OnGenerateTurret() method that we left empty at the beginning of this chapter while working on the level editor. Creating a turret is similar to creating other game objects in that we generate a new instance of the game object and pass our textures to it, along with the scrolling speed that is shared with the TerrainBackground class. Then, we position the turret just offscreen at the top and register for two events indicating that the turret is shooting bullets or has been hit so we can handle its death. Then, we add the object to the list of active game objects and to our turret list.

Let's now implement the _turret_OnTurretShoots event handler:

```
private void _turret_OnTurretShoots(object sender,
GameplayEvents.TurretShoots e)
{
    var bullet1 =
        new TurretBulletSprite(LoadTexture(TurretBulletTexture),
        e.Direction, e.Angle);
    bullet1.Position = e.Bullet1Position;
    bullet1.zIndex = -10;
```

```
var bullet2 =
    new TurretBulletSprite(LoadTexture(TurretBulletTexture),
    e.Direction, e.Angle);
bullet2.Position = e.Bullet2Position;
bullet2.zIndex = -10;

AddGameObject(bullet1);
AddGameObject(bullet2);

_turretBulletList.Add(bullet1);
_turretBulletList.Add(bullet2);
}
```

Here, we instantiate two TurretBulletSprite game objects using the info that was given to us by the TurretSprite object via the TurretShoots event. One notable thing that is new is the usage of the zIndex property of all our game objects. If you remember from the earlier chapters of this book, the zIndex represents the order in which we want to draw our objects. Since we want to make sure the turret bullets are drawn underneath the turret so they appear to fly out of the cannon barrels, we set a zIndex to -10, whereas the Turret has the default zIndex of zero. This will cause our main drawing function to draw the bullets first and then place the turret on top. We have not used the zIndex until now because we have not had a need for it.

We are ready to add our turret bullets to the code base. Create a new class called TurretBulletSprite in the Objects directory.

```
public class TurretBulletSprite : BaseGameObject
{
    private const float BULLET_SPEED = 18.0f;
    private Vector2 _bulletCenterPosition;

    public Segment CollisionSegment
    {
```

```
        get
        {
            var segment = _direction * _texture.Height;
            return new Segment(_position, Vector2.Add(
            _position, segment));
        }
    }

    public TurretBulletSprite(Texture2D texture, Vector2
    direction, float angle)
    {
        _texture = texture;
        _direction = direction;
        _direction.Normalize();

        _bulletCenterPosition = new Vector2(_texture.Width / 2,
        _texture.Height / 2);
        _angle = angle;
    }

    public void Update()
    {
        Position = Position + _direction * BULLET_SPEED;
    }

    public override void Render(SpriteBatch spriteBatch)
    {
        spriteBatch.Draw(_texture, _position, _texture.Bounds,
        Color.White, _angle,
                        _bulletCenterPosition, 1f,
                        SpriteEffects.None, 0f);
    }
}
```

There is not a lot of code here. The bullet is created with a texture, a direction, and an angle that will not change over time. The constructor normalizes the direction, just in case it is not normalized already, and then it calculates the center point of the bullet texture so we can rotate it when we draw it. The Update() method takes care of moving the bullet at high speed across the screen and the Render() method draws the bullet.

What remains is the CollisionSegment property, which we will use for detecting collisions with the player object.

Collision Detection

Since we decided not to use our Axis Aligned Bounding Box (AABB) collision detection algorithm, we had to use a different way to handle collisions. We have a few algorithm choices to pick from: we could use an Oriented Bounding Box (OBB) algorithm, a sphere/box collision strategy or detect the intersection between a line and an axis aligned bounding box. In the OBB algorithm, the oblique bounding boxes would be used by bullets, since they are almost always at an angle, and we would need to calculate the intersection of the bullets' oblique bounding boxes with the player sprite's axis aligned boxes. On the other hand, if we represented bullets as a small sphere near the center of the sprite, the collision detection algorithm would be very simple and efficient to compute. In the end, however, we decided to calculate the intersection between a segment and the player, which is a little more complex and a little less efficient than the sphere/AABB collision detection, but also a little more accurate.

So, what is a Segment? It is simply a line that has a starting location P1 and an end location P2 and is implemented like this:

```
public class Segment
{
    public Vector2 P1 { get; private set; }
    public Vector2 P2 { get; private set; }
```

```
public Segment(Vector2 p1, Vector2 p2)
{
    P1 = p1;
    P2 = p2;
}
}
```

So, when the TurretBulletSprite calculates its CollisionSegment, it multiplies the normalized _direction vector by the texture's height. This gives us a vector that is exactly as long as the bullet itself. Then, we create a Segment that starts at the bullet's position and ends at the texture heights, going in the right _direction.

To detect collisions, we'll implement a new SegmentAABBCollisionDetector class that works similarly to the AABBCollisionDetector, but works by finding if a segment intersects with an aligned axis bounding box. The algorithm is simple and similar to the AABB algorithm. If the starting point's X value of the segment is within the bounding box X values AND the point's Y value is within the bounding box Y values, then we have a collision. Then we do the same check for the point at the end of the segment. Here is the code:

```
public class SegmentAABBCollisionDetector<A>
    where A : BaseGameObject
{
    private A _passiveObject;

    public SegmentAABBCollisionDetector(A passiveObject)
    {
        _passiveObject = passiveObject;
    }
```

```
public void DetectCollisions(Segment segment, Action<A>
collisionHandler)
{
    if (DetectCollision(_passiveObject, segment))
    {
        collisionHandler(_passiveObject);
    }
}
public void DetectCollisions(List<Segment> segments,
Action<A> collisionHandler)
{
    foreach(var segment in segments)
    {
        if (DetectCollision(_passiveObject, segment))
        {
            collisionHandler(_passiveObject);
        }
    }
}

private bool DetectCollision(A passiveObject, Segment
segment)
{
    foreach(var activeBB in passiveObject.BoundingBoxes)
    {
        if (DetectCollision(segment.P1, activeBB) ||
            DetectCollision(segment.P2, activeBB))
        {
            return true;
        }
```

```
        else
        {
            return false;
        }
    }

    return false;
}
private bool DetectCollision(Vector2 p, BoundingBox bb)
{
    if (p.X < bb.Position.X + bb.Width &&
        p.X > bb.Position.X &&
        p.Y < bb.Position.Y + bb.Height &&
        p.Y > bb.Position.Y)
    {
        return true;
    }
    else
    {
        return false;
    }
}
}
```

We can now put all of this together in the GameplayState class. Add the following code to the DetectCollisions() class to add bullet and missile collisions to the turret so the player can destroy them, which is a key survival strategy:

```
var turretBulletCollisionDetector =
    new SegmentAABBCollisionDetector<PlayerSprite>(
    _playerSprite);
```

```
bulletCollisionDetector.DetectCollisions(_turretList, (bullet,
turret) =>
{
    var hitEvent = new GameplayEvents.ObjectHitBy(bullet);
    turret.OnNotify(hitEvent);
    _soundManager.OnNotify(hitEvent);
    bullet.Destroy();
});

missileCollisionDetector.DetectCollisions(_turretList,
(missile, turret) =>
{
    var hitEvent = new GameplayEvents.ObjectHitBy(missile);
    turret.OnNotify(hitEvent);
    _soundManager.OnNotify(hitEvent);
    missile.Destroy();
});
```

Then, in the same method, modify the `if (!_playerDead)` section to add the turret bullet collisions with the player:

```
if (!_playerDead)
{
    var segments = new List<Segment>();
    foreach (var bullet in _turretBulletList)
    {
        segments.Add(bullet.CollisionSegment);
    }
    turretBulletCollisionDetector.DetectCollisions(segments, _ =>
    {
        KillPlayer();
    });
```

```
playerCollisionDetector.DetectCollisions(_playerSprite,
(chopper, player) =>
{
    KillPlayer();
});
}
```

Cleaning Up

Now that everything is hooked up, we need to perform our usual cleaning.
When turrets are destroyed, they must be removed from the game. When
turrets and turret bullets are offscreen (but not when they have just been
added to the game and are just above the screen), they must be removed.
We will not cover this task here, but you can see how we handled that in
this chapter's end solution.

Adding Text

The last thing we want to add is game text to wish the player some good
luck when they start the level and to congratulate them when they clear the
level. For this, we will reuse our GameOverText object since the font is just
the right size. To make this happen, we just need to add a new text game
object and implement the last three level events that we left empty at the
beginning of this chapter:

```
private GameOverText _levelStartEndText;
public override void LoadContent()
{
    _levelStartEndText = new GameOverText(LoadFont(GameOverFont));
}
```

```
private void _level_OnLevelStart(object sender,
LevelEvents.StartLevel e)
{
    _levelStartEndText.Text = "Good luck, Player 1!";
    _levelStartEndText.Position = new Vector2(350, 300);
    AddGameObject(_levelStartEndText);
}

private void _level_OnLevelEnd(object sender, LevelEvents.
EndLevel e)
{
    _levelStartEndText.Text = "You escaped. Congrats!";
    _levelStartEndText.Position = new Vector2(300, 300);
    AddGameObject(_levelStartEndText);
}

private void _level_OnLevelNoRowEvent(object sender,
LevelEvents.NoRowEvent e)
{
    RemoveGameObject(_levelStartEndText);
}
```

This little bit of extra details really makes a nice difference to our game.

Reviewing Our Level Design

Our game now has the ability to load a level text file and play through it, but is our level challenging or fun to play? We would argue that it is challenging. As designed, this level is almost impossible to beat because the turrets are brutal and incredibly difficult to deal with. Also, very early in the level we have four turrets on the screen at the same time and it is very difficult to move beyond that point.

Thankfully, it is straightforward to fix this issue by editing Level1.txt and changing the location of turrets to make the level easier.

As we played our own level after the turrets were added, we realized that they added an element of surprise to the player, who then thinks that things really get serious. The game is not joking around and will kill them if they make just a single mistake. That element of surprise, combined with seeing four turrets at the same time come into view, caused us to frown and really focus. The game became fun!

Try to update the Level1.txt file to add or remove turrets, or change the number of enemy choppers generated, or when they get generated, then run the game and see how it plays through. If you keep dying, however, but still want to see the level through the end, we added a _indestructible variable in the BaseGameState. When set to true, the player will not die.

Improving the Gameplay

As we were working on the code for this chapter, it became obvious that there was a little bit of stuttering in the gameplay, with the sprites not moving smoothly across the screen. There are many factors that can cause a game to stutter. MonoGame tries to run as efficiently as possible, and by default, it will call the Update() function 60 times per second. However, certain things can cause the game to miss drawing a frame every now and then. The usual culprit is the .Net garbage collector doing work removing instances of objects from memory when they are not referenced anymore. We do have some room for improvement here. For every Update() call, we deactivate enemy objects that are off the screen and leave them in memory. Eventually, the garbage collector will pick them up. The improvements we could make here would involve having a pool of pre-instantiated objects and recycle game objects the same way we have been recycling our particle objects in Chapter 8.

However, in our case, the stuttering was occurring even when the garbage collector was not working so the problem must be somewhere else. The Update() and Draw() functions together must not take longer than 1/60th of a second to run; otherwise, we will not be able to achieve 60 frames per second. In that case, MonoGame responds by setting a GameTime.IsRunningSlowly flag to true to allow the developer to react. It will also skip calling the Draw() function a few times to be able to call Update() within the time frame can hopefully catch up. This would cause the game to look jerky, but this is not our problem. While we could add a counter in our GameplayState class that we increment at every call to Render() and display the number of frames per seconds on the screen, we are fairly confident that our game runs well below the time constraints.

Another factor that can cause stuttering is how MonoGame synchronizes with the refresh rate of your monitor when it tries to draw things to the screen because ultimately we cannot redraw the screen more often than the monitor can handle. While this is a deeper topic for the scope of this book, we have found that telling MonoGame not to synchronize with the monitor resulted in a smoother experience.

We adjusted the Main() function in our Program class to tell MonoGame to use a fixed time step by setting the game.IsFixedTimeStep flag to true, which forces the game to run at a specific number of frames per second. Because we still want to run the game at 60 frames per seconds, we must tell MonoGame how long each frame takes, which is 1000 milliseconds divided by 60. Our Program's Main() function now looks like this:

```
static void Main()
{
    using (var game = new MainGame(WIDTH, HEIGHT, new
    SplashState()))
    {
        game.IsFixedTimeStep = true;
```

```
    game.TargetElapsedTime = TimeSpan.
    FromMilliseconds(1000.0f / 60);
    game.Run();
  }
}
```

Then, to turn off the synchronization with the monitor, we set the graphics.SynchronizeWithVerticalRetrace flag to false in MainGame's Initialize() method:

```
graphics.SynchronizeWithVerticalRetrace = false;
```

With those things in place, the game started running much smoother.

Summary

In this chapter, we learned how to create a grid-like internal representation of a level and how to load data from a text file into this grid. We also implemented a Level class that can use this internal grid of level events and cause actual game objects to be added to the screen. Finally, we added turrets that can shoot the player, which has been the most difficult game object to implement yet, involving rotations and vectors and a new way to detect collisions between segments and axis aligned boxes. We did a lot of work here and our game looks much better.

While this is the final chapter of the book, our journey into game development is just getting started. Game development is really a collection of techniques and algorithms that are stitched together to form a game and there is a lot more to discover. For example, we used zIndices to determine the drawing order of our objects, but there are layering techniques out there, where anything that a player can collide with is drawn at a lower layer, while the player and enemies are drawn at a higher layer. We have also barely scratched the surface of particle engines. We did not add the ability to have our textures morph as they age! And what about path detection and AI agents to allow our game objects to act independently from the gameplay state?

There is a lot more to learn, but this book gives you a good foundation and a good starting point to build games with MonoGame. So what will you add to our game? Here are just a few possibilities that you could tackle next:

- More background elements like rivers and bridges, or city landscapes.

- A wider variety of enemies.

- Boss fights!

- Adding different weapons to the players.

- When enemies die, they could generate consumable game objects that give the player some kind of boost if they pick them up, like power ups.

We look forward to playing the game that you will build in the future!

Index

A

Aligned axis bounding box (AABB), 195, 196, 307

Animations
  downsides, 246, 247
  engine
    AddFrame method, 254
    algorithm, 252
    AnimationFrame class, 249
    classes, 249
    class variables, 250
    computing option, 252
    looping, 253
    ReverseAnimation, 255
    source code, 252, 253
  fighter plane
    frames, 256
    GameplayInput Command, 261
    PlayerSprite class, 256, 257
    StopMoving() method, 258, 259
    Update() method, 260
  sprite sheets, 243–245
  state machines, 246–248
  text
    content pipeline tool, 263
    fonts, 262
    game objects, 264–266
    game over, 267–270
    tracking lives, 266, 267
  texture atlases, 244, 245
  two-dimensional games, 242

Architecture
  desktop template, 44–46
  execution order, 49
  game class, 38, 39
  MainGame.cs file, 45–49
  pipeline app, 35–38
  rendered pixels, solution/project, 40–43

Artificial intelligence (AI), 53

Asset pipeline, 75
  agile process, 78
  asset loading/unloading, 79
  asset optimizations/ targeting, 76
  BaseGameState class, 79–81
  benefits, 76
  ContentManager class, 76, 77
  MainGame class, 81

Printed in the United States
by Book savers

Printed in the United States
By Bookmasters